WHEN THEY WERE MINE

WHEN THEY WERE MINE

Memories of a Branch Davidian Wife and Mother

by

Sheila Martin

as told to Catherine Wessinger

BAYLOR UNIVERSITY PRESS

Cover Design: Andrew Brozyna, ab design

Cover Photo: The Martin Family. Photo courtesy of Sheila Martin. Used by permission.

Interior photos, courtesy of Sheila Martin and Catherine Wessinger. Used by permission.

Interior illustrations drawn by Sheila Martin. Used by permission.

Library of Congress Cataloging-in-Publication Data

Martin, Sheila, 1947-
  When they were mine : memoirs of a Branch Davidian wife and mother / Sheila Martin ; as told to Catherine Wessinger.
     p. cm.
  Includes bibliographical references and index.
  ISBN 978-1-60258-000-8 (pbk. : alk. paper)
  1. Martin, Sheila, 1947- 2. Branch Davidians--Biography. 3. Waco Branch Davidian Disaster, Tex., 1993. I. Wessinger, Catherine Lowman. II. Title.
  BP605.B72M37 2009
  976.4'284063092--dc22
  [B]

                                        2008029711

Printed in the United States of America on acid-free paper with a minimum of 30% pcw recycled content.

This book is dedicated to my mother,
Muriel Elizabeth Wheaton,
who has loved me all my life,
and
Joseph and Helen Martin and family,
who have borne a great burden,
and
all who have helped in my *going home*.
—Sheila Martin—

TABLE OF CONTENTS

FOREWORD

I met Sheila Martin on February 23, 2001, on my first trip
to Waco. I and some other scholars were attending a conference at Baylor University in Waco hosted by the J. M. Dawson Institute of Church-State Studies and presenting papers
there on new religious movements and religious liberty in
America.[1] Sociologist Stuart A. Wright of Lamar University
in Beaumont, Texas, made arrangements for some of the surviving Branch Davidians to come and meet with us after the
conference. The Branch Davidians and some of the scholars
subsequently adjourned to Waco's Cracker Barrel restaurant
for further discussions.

The next day, Sheila Martin, accompanied by her daughter Kimberly, gave Susan J. Palmer and me a ride out to
Mount Carmel, the site of the Branch Davidians' residence
that became so famous in 1993 when it was the focus of a
fifty-one-day siege by federal agents. The siege culminated in
a tank and CS gas assault carried out by FBI agents, which
resulted in a fire that killed seventy-six Branch Davidians

including twenty-three children. Sheila's husband and four oldest children died in the fire. We joined the other visiting scholars, who were given a tour of Mount Carmel by Sheila Martin, Clive Doyle, his mother Edna Doyle, Catherine Matteson, David Koresh's mother, Bonnie Haldeman, and her husband, Roy Haldeman, and groundskeeper Ron Goins. On the drive out to Mount Carmel, Sheila shared that she thought that Branch Davidian women's voices should be heard more. I certainly agreed and at that time I wondered whether I could facilitate that.

I had already written *How the Millennium Comes Violently: From Jonestown to Heaven's Gate*, which contains an extensive chapter on the Branch Davidian case. After returning to New Orleans I sent copies of the book to Sheila, Bonnie, Catherine, and Clive.[2]

I got to know Sheila and Kimberly Martin, Bonnie Haldeman, and Clive Doyle a little better when they came to New Orleans on February 10, 2002, for the appeal of their wrongful death lawsuit against the government being heard in the United States Court of Appeals for the Fifth Circuit.[3]

I was back in Texas twice in 2003. David Tabb Stewart of Southwestern University in Georgetown, Texas, organized a symposium on "Waco: Ten Years After" to correspond with the tenth anniversary of the raid conducted by agents of the Bureau of Alcohol, Tobacco, and Firearms (ATF) on February 28, 1993, which erupted into a shootout that killed four ATF agents and five Branch Davidians, wounded many, and precipitated the fifty-one-day siege. A sixth Branch Davidian was shot and killed by ATF agents later that day as he attempted to return to Mount Carmel on foot. Guest scholars James T. Richardson, Stuart A. Wright, and I, along with David Tabb

Stewart and his students, attended a memorial service in the new chapel at Mount Carmel on February 28, 2003.[4]

I returned to Mount Carmel on April 19, 2003, for the tenth anniversary memorial service commemorating the fire and all those who died at Mount Carmel in 1993. While I was there, I resolved to devote my 2004–2005 sabbatical to collecting the oral histories of Sheila Martin, Bonnie Haldeman, Clive Doyle, and Catherine Matteson, if they would permit it. I drove back to Waco in August 2003 to ask them if I could interview them extensively during my sabbatical, and they agreed.

Sheila Martin's autobiography is based on four ninety-minute audiotapes recorded on March 9 and 10, 2004; a fifth interview in February 2006 about the meaning of her drawings (see the appendix); and a sixth interview recorded in April 2007. In 2004, on the very first night that we got together in her living room, Sheila immediately spoke about the traumatic experiences of 1993 when her husband, Douglas Wayne ("Wayne") Martin (42), and their four oldest children, Wayne Joseph Martin (20), Anita Marie Martin (18), Sheila Renee Martin (15), and Lisa Marie Martin (13), died in the fire that consumed the residence at Mount Carmel. Sheila had come out earlier in the siege hoping to be rejoined with her three youngest children who had been sent out, Jamie Martin (11), who had been severely handicapped by meningitis, Daniel Martin (6), and Kimberly Martin (4). Jamie subsequently died in 1998. Sheila wanted to speak of her experience of these traumatic events and her feelings about them in our interviews.

Sheila then suggested that we continue the interview while on a drive the next day from Waco to Six Flags over Texas in

Fort Worth along with her daughter Kimberly. They wanted to pick up some season passes at Six Flags. I was surprised at the idea, but it worked out perfectly. It was raining that day. With the windshield wipers going, I drove, while asking Sheila questions about her life, and Sheila spoke into my small tape recorder. The rain stopped long enough for us to enjoy a brief visit to Six Flags, including a memorable experience on the Sponge Bob ride. We continued the interview on the drive back to Waco, again in the rain. The trip to Six Flags was exactly the fun break we all needed from complete immersion in Sheila's story of her keenly felt loss of loved ones. The interviews were concluded back in Waco.

Sheila reports that her mother was always busy and always moving around. Sheila is a lot like that herself. She constantly has a project going to improve her house. She works hard to provide a nice home for her children and herself. I have assumed that she learned her construction skills while living at Mount Carmel and participating in David Koresh's building projects. Sheila loves taking care of her children, and Daniel and Kimberly will soon be out on their own. She also loves taking care of the small children in her charge at the Christian daycare center where she works. Sheila loves to nurture life and growth, whether it is her plants, animals, the children at the daycare center, or her own children. Sheila values life.

I am impressed with Sheila's spirituality. She trusts in God's grace and love. She is keenly appreciative of the small blessings of daily life, including the interest and kindness of people who have helped her, her family, and the other Branch Davidian survivors after the fire. I have learned that the Branch Davidians at Mount Carmel were a large, unconventional family and that the sense of kinship among the survivors remains strong. Sheila wants the general public to get to know her immediate family members and the Branch Davidians as real people; those who died in 1993 were human beings who are missed by their loved ones. This is the reason she is publishing this autobiography.

The Methodology

The audiotapes recorded in 2004, 2006, and 2007 were transcribed by several assistants and corrected by me. The initial copyediting was done by Alanda Wraye, and I did the final copyediting and arranging. Sheila Martin proofread the manuscript three times making additions and corrections. Sheila gave me the title, *When They Were Mine*, on one of my visits to Waco.

I visited Waco in December 2005 to scan Sheila's family photographs and in February 2006 to photograph her drawings, a number of which are included in this book.

This autobiography is in Sheila Martin's own words. Grammar has been corrected throughout, but not extensively to preserve the spoken nature of Sheila's account. I have added footnotes to provide context and further information about the events and people that Sheila discusses.

Acknowledgments

I thank Sharon Orgeron, Erin Proven, Deborah Halter, and Alanda Wraye for their care in transcribing the audiotapes. I am grateful to Alanda Wraye, who has ably served as editorial assistant. Without her work and interest, this project would have taken much longer to complete. I thank my son, Clinton Wessinger, for serving as my technical assistant in converting the audiotapes to digital files.

I thank Loyola University New Orleans for a grant that paid for part of my travel costs to Waco, and for the Rev. H. James Yamauchi, S.J. Professorship in the History of Religions, which since 2006 helps to fund my continued Branch Davidian research. I am very grateful to my parents, Bryson and Ellen Lowman, for a financial gift that supported my sabbatical, and also paid for transcribing and the initial copyediting. I thank them for all their love and support.

I am grateful for the vision of Carey Newman, director of Baylor University Press, in publishing this second Branch Davidian autobiography; and to Diane Smith, production manager; and Jay Bruce, the Baylor University Press copyeditor, for their expert and professional handling of the manuscript.

Most of all I thank Sheila Martin for so generously sharing her life's story with me. It is a privilege to know her.

Catherine Wessinger

PURPOSE OF THIS BOOK

The most important thing I want the readers of this book to know is that there were people at Mount Carmel with David Koresh, who were living lives every day, who had the same hopes, dreams, wishes, and desires as everyone else to do well. They believed in God. They wanted to please God and the people around them. They wanted to be able to learn how to love more—to love not only themselves, but the people around them, and first of all, to love God. We knew everything else would trickle down from loving God first. Once we had a true understanding and love for God, we could do everything else, whether it's waiting, or going through times when things are not always good. The people at Mount Carmel just wanted to have a chance to be alive, just to wake up and say: "It's a new day. No matter what happened yesterday I can do better today. With God's help, I can be nicer to a person than I was the day before. If they weren't nice to me, I can show them I can still love them no matter what the situation."

I feel the government took that away from the people who died at Mount Carmel.[5] The little babies and the young people, especially, were robbed of a chance to even have a choice about how to live their lives. The adults made the choice to come to Mount Carmel to read and study the Bible; they should have had it.

There's this other thought that stays in the back of my mind. While we were inside Mount Carmel with the federal agents outside, David said they were obeying their commanders. They needed to do what they were told to do. David said that we should strive to have that same relationship with God. Sometimes God sends a better understanding of how to obey him to people who are open to it. Sometimes God puts these people in a strange place. It happened many times in the Bible, and David said maybe it's happening again.

When we were in Palestine,[6] David said all we had to do was get up, eat the food that was provided, and read our Bibles, but we made choices to do other things and not to use our time wisely for God. Then we got to Mount Carmel and really started working.[7] It seemed like there was never an end to the work. Then this situation occurred in 1993 when the federal agents came and people died. We didn't need that. We didn't want it. It wasn't something we would have ever thought was going to happen. Yet under certain circumstances we were willing to accept whatever God chose to do for us, including our deaths. We just didn't know how it would happen, and we didn't want it to be in such a horrible way.

I want people to know that there were families at Mount Carmel, people who loved each other, who wanted the best for each other, and who most of all wanted God.

EARLY LIFE IN BOSTON

I was born in March 1947 in Boston, Massachusetts, a city where history abounds. I lived and experienced it all in the early part of my life. The different lifestyles, the museums and universities, and the neighborhoods, all have influenced me in so many ways. I didn't realize that no matter how far away I moved from my birthplace I would be forever linked by not only family ties but also by a date that I celebrated every year until I left Boston at age 22. The date is April 19! I celebrated it as a holiday from school, Patriot's Day, and I noted the Boston Marathon's popularity and importance in our country and the world. I was always surprised at how it could snow so late in April. I even remember memorizing the "Midnight Ride of Paul Revere," and can still repeat it.[8]

But what happened on April 19, 1993—the day I will never forget until Christ comes again—made the date take on a very different meaning. Now I associate that day with the deaths of my friends and the deaths of my dear husband and four beautiful children. Deaths so horrible, so utterly horrible, that to have to wonder how they looked when it was all over for them that day becomes unbearable. Sometimes now in all the hustle and bustle of life, I can almost forget, but then I only have to look at their pictures and all the feelings of that day in April come back.

My mother, Muriel Elizabeth West Wheaton, and my dad, Harold Charles Wheaton, had six children, three boys and three girls. I was the first of the three girls.

My mother was born in Cambridge, Massachusetts, of parents from Danville, Virginia, and Providence, Rhode Island. The racial lines in her family included white, Native

American, and African heritage. It meant many cultures in one family, many different complexions and facial features ranging from very white to very dark and all in-between.

My father's family was from Nova Scotia and included African, Native American, and French and English people. Recently I read of a book that speaks of slave families that left America with the British after fighting with them against the Americans in the Revolutionary War. After the war ended the black families went to live in Nova Scotia. I couldn't believe my eyes. I had told people all my life that my father's family came from there, and now I was learning how they came to be living there. I then realized where the defiant part of me comes from. Perhaps that is what helped me to make a break from my religious background toward a new religion, even though I had to stand alone.

My mother had a brother and two sisters. My father had a big family—maybe there were five brothers and a sister. So we had a big family life and most of us were in the Episcopal Church. I grew up thinking in more of a Catholic mode because the Episcopal church we attended was high church.

My mom was always busy, moving around. Until a few years ago, she had very dark hair. I remember her standing at the stove curling her hair with a little curling iron. She still does that. I am glad I have all these little memories of my family.

I was happy. We did not worry too much about what things we had. We just kind of accepted things as they were.

My earliest memories are of living on the second floor of my maternal grandmother's house. We knew her as "Mama." She had left grandpa and eventually bought a couple of houses. My father and mother, along with their children, were occupying the second floor of her house in the Roxbury section of Boston. My grandmother, my mother's brother and sister and her sister's two children lived on the third floor. A German couple lived on the first floor. I remember only one other child of color on my street. Some of our relatives, some older and some younger, lived on a few streets around us. The children on our little street attended the elementary school next to our house. We moved away when I was seven.

Our next neighborhood was in the Franklin Field projects. We were the only family of color in our apartment house. These were much nicer projects than the ones across the city. I found out later that there were many cousins living in the back of the project area.

The neighborhood was changing from predominantly Jewish to a Christian neighborhood, with some parts dominated by Irish Catholics. From the fourth through the sixth grades, I was one of only thirty Christian children who attended school on the Jewish Holy Days, which were observed by the Jewish children at my elementary school. This was a very large school in a highly populated area of the city. We also saw the Jewish children attending Hebrew School across the street every afternoon. I realize now that God was preparing me for an understanding of a lifestyle that I would adopt myself much later on.

We lived at the Franklin Field projects for four years. My father, a master plumber, did not work as I feel he should have. My mother took up the banner of working to support the family. There were no school buses or rides in the family car to school. We walked many long roads to school early each morning. Even though we were on our own so much, I know God was taking care of us. I remember arriving very early one morning at school when I was in the third grade. The teachers let me in because it was cold. They gave me milk and Saltine crackers. That was my breakfast. I appreciate so very much their care and concern. I don't tell this story because I was being neglected, but to illustrate how resilient we were as children. God was surely looking over us. I've not forgotten the taste of that simple breakfast.

I was preparing to attend junior high school in a district I knew was going to be a challenge, primarily because of my race, when I was told we would be moving again. We moved to Lawrence Avenue in the Dorchester area of Boston. My mother still lives there. After being in the previous neighborhood with mostly Jewish people, where I was just one of about thirty Christian kids in school, we moved to a neighborhood that was mostly black. In the seventh grade I was meeting new people, trying to adjust to a whole new life—everything was different.

My school again was next door to my grandmother's house. When we moved there our aunt and cousins were living above us again. This time we were on the first floor. Eventually my grandma, my mother's brother, and a handyman moved into the second floor.

A year later my aunt and her family moved to California and that left the third-floor apartment vacant. We were told a family from New York was moving in. One day in August of 1963 I watched four children climb the front steps. My first reaction was to hope the family would hire me as a babysitter. Then I saw five adults walking behind them. I realized that with that many adults they wouldn't need me for babysitting, but God still would have me involved in their lives and they in mine. I was about to enter the twelfth grade and I was looking forward to what all it meant about being a senior in high school. I guess I felt it would be a year of being my own person, becoming an adult.

BECOMING A BRANCH DAVIDIAN SEVENTH-DAY ADVENTIST

The new people who came to live on the third floor of my grandmother's house were Davidians. They were members of three families but they all used the last name "ben David." One of them was a man named John Ramsey. I became friends with Nina, who was five years older than me, and her mother. They decided one day in October 1963 to invite us upstairs and let us see what kind of food they had. They were vegetarians. We used to see them go out on Saturday mornings. They said that they were going to church. I could not understand why they were going to church on Saturday. That October during the Feast of Tabernacles they invited us up for a meal. Later they invited me to the Seventh-day Adventist church.

I did not know why they called themselves Davidian Seventh-day Adventists. I did not realize that they were learning things different from other Seventh-day Adventists.[9] I did not know how this would affect me in the future and how I would always feel left out of the mainstream of life because I was part of a different sect in the church.

The people upstairs were very nice. When there were programs at the church they would invite our family. I remember talking to my mother about what they were discussing at their Bible meetings and what they were saying about their religion. When I went with them to church I saw some books there that looked like some of the same books that were in my house. I said, "Ma, I saw these books at the church and they are the same books that I have been reading all of my life." She said, "Oh, I had a friend Lavinia, who was a Seventh-day Adventist." She had never told me. I never knew anything about it, but Lavinia had sold my mother some books from the Seventh-day Adventist Church. I loved reading those books. They were books of Bible stories, such as *Uncle Albert's Bible Stories*.

I was fascinated that my mother had an Adventist friend but never really knew anything about Adventism. She never had an inkling about the Seventh-day Adventist church in Boston. At that time we were just going back and forth between churches. We were going to the Catholic church down the road because it was easier to walk to it than get on the bus and go all the way to the Episcopal church, and the Catholic church was similar to what we did in the Episcopal church. In the Catholic church I had the feeling that I was part of something special. Everyone I knew thought it was the best church.

When Nina and her family started telling us about the Bible, they said to look at the calendar: the week starts on Sunday and ends on Saturday. If you are going to go by the calendar, it shows that at the end of six days you are to worship. When someone would say, "things have changed," I would say there are still seven days in a week and at the end of six days you are to worship. The truth was plain to see.

One Saturday my mother and I walked to the Seventh-day Adventist church, because we had been invited by the Davidians. As we walked to church that day I told my mother about the seventh-day Sabbath. She mostly said that it was not the church that she grew up in and she did not want to change. She felt that I should not want to change, but I didn't see a problem in doing so.

Little by little other things came up. As the ben David family told me more things, I studied for myself. The main thing was the calendar and its seven days. That was the main thing that kept me believing. I read more of the Bible. I tried to see how all of these things worked, and started putting more and more Bible truths together. They appeared to make common sense.

By then I was getting to the end of high school and becoming friends with some other people. They were inviting me to come to their homes. That began to become a conflict, whether to go to their homes on a Friday night or to go upstairs to have Bible study with the Davidians. I did go one Friday to visit friends but I kept thinking of the Bible study I was missing. When I graduated from high school my mother told me that my aunt wanted me to come spend the summer with her in New York City. I realize now that they were trying to get me away from the things I was thinking about in terms of changing my beliefs and my life.

When I came back at the end of the summer the Davidians were still living upstairs. I told Nina I was planning to go to computer school in January. She called me up one day and said the place where she worked needed to hire people. I asked, "What kind of a place is it?" She said it was a hat factory. I said, "A factory! I am not going to work in a factory." She said, "Well, this is October. You start school in January. You could work for a couple of months." She made sense, so I did just that. I was about to begin a life I never realized. It was my first adult job. I made one dollar an hour. I thought

I had a lot of money. Even though it wasn't what I wanted, I enjoyed the work.

I remember Nina used to bring sandwiches to eat at work. One day I did not have money or lunch, and she offered me one of her sandwiches. I asked, "What kind of sandwich is it?" She said, "Honey and peanut butter." Her bread was rye bread. I did not think I'd like that. She said, "Why don't you just try it?" Well, I liked it. It was delicious. She said if I liked it, she would bring me some more. After that I started buying my own rye bread and other food, concentrating on not eating pork.

Little by little, sitting there with Nina every day on the train and buses, we saw each other more and she told me more things about her faith. We became close. We were like sisters. I was there every day listening to what she had to say about different things. Little by little, I realized I did not want to eat pork and beef. I would not eat all the things available in the store.[10] Little by little that caused some conflict with my mother. I no longer wanted to eat the things that my mother was accustomed to fixing for me. My mother began to see that associating with Nina was changing my lifestyle. I was upstairs with the ben Davids more often. My younger sister used to go up there, too. After a while my younger sister stopped coming up. She was almost five years younger than me. I often wondered why she didn't continue. It would have been nice to have a family member with me.

I was working with Nina every day and then some time that March I decided I was not going to work there any longer. I still had the connection with the ben David family, I was still learning things, and my mother had the feeling I was getting further and further away from all the things that she believed in. Eventually, my mother became unhappy with the people upstairs and started to say to them, "You are trying to take my daughter away from me." I did not see that. I just saw it as a situation where I was able to learn things and it was okay with me. I was learning things, meeting people, and seeing places that I had never seen before.

After a while I did not see Nina as much, even though they still lived upstairs. I was working and traveling in a different direction. I remember there was a time when there was some sort of conflict going on upstairs. I did not understand it. This is when Brother Roden was sending literature to the house. They were learning about this new part of the message, and they were having arguments about it. Eventually they split up, and Nina moved down the street to another apartment with her mother and John Ramsey to learn the new truths together. I did not see Nina as much then, although I would visit. Little by little I was trying to make up my mind about what I wanted. Did I want to be a Seventh-day Adventist or an Episcopalian? Did I want to stay with my mother and her beliefs? How was I going to live my life?

One day I went with my mother to a birthday party for the son of a family friend. I said, "I am not going to eat any meat." The Adventists and Davidians were all vegetarians and Nina and her mother had been trying to get me to give up eating meat altogether. They did not even eat fish. I had learned about pork, and then beef, and then about the types of fish. I learned about the clean and unclean foods. I was trying to make up my mind there at the party. I remember going up into the kitchen and they were out of the appetizers they were serving. Just as I thought, "Good, I do not have to worry," the hostess brought out a whole new tray of pigs in a blanket![11]

When I went home that night I felt I was really going to make up my mind. It was not easy to say, "I am not going to do this, and I will do that."

I understand the struggles that I hear people have with their children. I think I am more patient with my own children because of my experience of trying to do the right things as a teenager. I do not have the burden of thinking my children are not going to believe, or they are going to give it up. I believe that God will make it possible at some point that they will know what they want, they will understand the Bible, and God will help them. I have that comfort.

I went to Nina's place the next day and said, "Yes, I want to visit with all of you more and become a Seventh-day Adventist." I had learned that it was necessary to be in the environment of constant prayer and Bible study to succeed.

I had a chance to go to school to be a dental assistant. John Ramsey and Nina came to see me the night before I was to leave to tell me not to forget what I had learned at the Bible meetings. They said, you do not want to go to this school and forget what you have learned about God. Then I really did not want to go. I was concerned that the school would make me lose track of what I had learned about the Bible from them. I had seen many times how easily I could go off and not see them as much. I decided not to go to the dental school. The ironic thing was that later Nina ended up going to school to become a dental assistant. She eventually gave up being a Branch Davidian and became mainly a Seventh-day Adventist. I believe that would have happened to me and I would have lost out on this whole experience. All these long stories and different situations show how things change.

I worked at several jobs for a while. In the meantime, Nina and I met some people from New Jersey who were Branch Davidians. We went to New Jersey for a camp meeting. On the weekend after the camp meeting we stayed at a hotel in Newark. One of the young men at the hotel was with the Branch Davidians. We worked for his brother, also a Branch Davidian, for a couple of days doing filing. We talked with this young man each day, and one day he left a note for me. I think this was the beginning of things changing between Nina and me. She asked, how come he left a note for you? She had met him first and expected a different attitude toward her.

While we were at the hotel, riots broke out in Newark. It is so strange to have been in that situation of violence and shooting, never imagining I would experience the same thing again. One night we were in our room. They told us to get away from the windows and to stay down on the floor. We couldn't leave the city. We couldn't get on a bus to go back to Boston for a while. I remember going downstairs the next day. There were soldiers in the lobby with guns.

If anyone had told me then, you will go through this again, law enforcement agents will be there, and people will be shooting at windows, I never would have believed it.

After the riot, the young man went back to his home in another state and Nina and I got on the bus to Boston. Nina and I ended up not being as friendly because of the situation with this young man. We were still talking and believing all the same things, but there was this little rift. Eventually he married someone else. At that point I went to California.

I spent two months with my aunt and cousins in California. I was there through August, possibly going into the beginning of September. While in California I attended a Seventh-day Adventist church. I went up to San Francisco. I was enjoying living in California. I was thinking perhaps I would stay there, maybe I would find some other Adventists, some other Davidians. I spoke to Nina on the phone and she asked, "Are you coming back for the Atonement? Are you going to be back for any of the Holy Days?" However she said it, I thought maybe I should at least go back and observe the Holy Days with the believers. At my aunt's house I was trying to understand how to be a Branch Davidian and at the same time live in a different environment and not give it up. So when Nina asked, "Aren't you going to come back?" I felt impressed to leave. I had not meant to leave so quickly, but Nina's mentioning all these things made me want to go back. I felt that those feast days were more important than anything else.

I went back and celebrated the High Holy Days. Then it was time for me to start looking for a job again. Eventually I got a job at a shoe factory. I worked in the office as a secretary for one of the buyers. I could buy shoes, stockings, and purses at discounted prices. This became a good job for me and for people in my family. They could come and pick out something, and I'd buy it for them. So this job was working out nicely.

I got a job there for Nina doing keypunching. Every day Nina and I went off to a health food store to buy lunch. We were going back to our situation of being friendly, being able to study more, and being a part of the Branch truth. During that time I was living at my great-aunt's house in Cambridge.

We talked about going to Waco to meet the people at Mount Carmel. We were going to raise some money to get bus tickets. Even if we had to hitchhike, we were going to try to get down to Texas. We told people we were going to go to school in Texas.

I left the job with the shoe company and began working at Traveler's Insurance Company as a typist. When I was working at Traveler's Insurance, I still studied with Nina, her brothers, and her mother. The Branch Davidian who was teaching us was John Ramsey, who came to visit from New Hampshire. When he was not there, we had Bible studies on our own, and other times we would go to a Seventh-day Adventist church.

There were times when we were very strict into one thing, and then kind of backsliding in other things, trying to feel like we were as other Adventists. We went off to an Adventist college one Sabbath afternoon with some of the Adventists, even though we were Branch Davidians. We wanted to be a part of them and were trying to feel like we were fitting in, that we were not so different in the things that we believed. It was not wanting to give up our differences with the Adventists, but wanting to have a chance to have some fun. We wanted people to accept our beliefs in the Bible even though it was not a popular truth with the Seventh-day Adventists.

We Branch Davidians are those "offshoot people" according to the Seventh-day Adventists. We believe in a kingdom on Earth before going to heaven. Adventists believe Christ will come from heaven in the clouds and we will meet him in the air. Adventists believe that when the lion and the lamb lie down together and the lion will eat straw like the ox (Isaiah 11:6-7), this will occur in heaven. But Branch Davidians believe that heaven has only green grass; straw is a dead food. Therefore the lion and the lamb lying down and eating straw together means this will happen on Earth.

INCREASING INDEPENDENCE: MOVING
TO NEW YORK CITY

Nina and I and two male friends were going back and forth from Boston to New York City to attend Seventh-day Adventist conferences and youth gatherings. These two friends treated us as any other people who believed in the Adventist truth, although they knew we were Branch Davidians.

I was 21 and started thinking I would like to move away from Boston. I was meeting more people in New York City and my aunt and cousins lived there. I had met some people from New York who came to the Boston Adventist church for a concert. They told me they went to a certain church in New York City. I felt I would like to visit them. I found out I could transfer with Traveler's Insurance to a job in New York City.

I started thinking of leaving Boston, but I felt my mother was not going to want me to go, even though at 21 you feel you can do what you want. Most people at that age move away.

I talked to my cousins in New York City and asked if I could come stay for a couple of days. They said yes. So I was getting all of these little chances to relocate to New York City. Plus my cousin's apartment was just across the street from a Seventh-day Adventist church. I got the job transfer with Traveler's and I started work there in July 1970.

What I was doing was very normal for someone my age. I wanted to meet new people and do new things. I told my mother I was going to New York City, but I did not tell her until I got there that I was going to live in New York. I still remember my mother crying on the phone. So many times later I thought of how badly I felt about not letting her know my whole plan. I told her, "Everyone wants to meet someone and get married and start a family." Staying at your mother's house when you are ten years old you cannot imagine going away from home, but when you are 21, you feel that is the most normal thing to do.

Later I went to stay with friends in Brooklyn whom I had met on previous visits. I stayed at a couple of places here, a couple of places there. At some point I saw my aunt. She was very strict. She did not know why I wanted to leave Boston, and she thought New York City was too rough for me. But my connection with New York City began in all the years that my parents took us to visit our cousins. Little by little, ever since I was young perhaps God was bringing me there. (Sometimes I think of how when I was visiting the Bronx as a child, Wayne was growing up in another part of New York City. He knew my cousin from one of his classes in college. She met him before I did.)

I look back on all the things that influenced me: the Adventist books, going to an elementary school with Jewish children and learning about the Holy Days they observed, and moving to the house my grandmother owned. When we moved into our apartment in my grandmother's house there was a Jewish reminder of God on all of the doors. I think they would touch it as they came in and went out. It was stuck right to the doorframe.[12] All these things were giving me little insights and more understanding as I learned about the Branch Davidian message and about the Sabbath. I know God wanted my family and me to move to my grandmother's house. The Davidians came to live there and taught us about Seventh-day Adventism. I know that God wanted to reveal to me his truth for the last days.

MEETING WAYNE MARTIN

In New York City I went to an Adventist church where I saw a young woman Delores, whom I had met earlier at an Adventist campground. Delores and her husband invited me to their home for a meal. I told them I was in New York City to stay. A month later I ended up at the Adventist church that my husband had attended since he was a little boy. Wayne was a fifth-generation Seventh-day Adventist. His grandfather was an Adventist pastor, and his family members were teachers in the Adventist school.

First, I attended the Adventist church in Brooklyn every week where I knew some people who had visited Boston. They had taken me to New York City a couple of times. I was meeting people in the Brooklyn church and people who lived in different places and people who knew the same people I knew. All this was what drew me to move to New York City.

After starting the job with Traveler's Insurance, I got a room in an apartment with a family from Jamaica in the Ebbets Field apartments, which used to be the Ebbets Field ballpark. I was living with a young woman, her husband and baby, and her sister and grandmother. I was learning all about their food and culture. We went to the Adventist church in Brooklyn. I was getting settled into Brooklyn when my friend Delores said that her real church was in St. Albans, a section in Queens. We went to the St. Albans Adventist church a month after I arrived in New York. I felt very much at home. A common truth of the Sabbath binds you to others in the faith.

In the afternoon I went back to the St. Albans Adventist church for the youth meetings. I went downstairs, and there was a piano with some people singing. A choir was getting ready to practice. There was a young man sitting at the piano.

All I could see was the back of his head. He was waiting for the people to get together. I asked, "Who is that over there?" My friend Mary told me his name was Wayne Martin. He did not turn around so I couldn't see his face, but I was still interested in him.

I went back that evening to hear the choir and some special music. When Wayne came out of the church, I told him I enjoyed the music he played that night. He said, "Thank you." Then I turned around and started to walk away. He came up to me and started talking. I told him who I was and that I knew Mary. I was still living in Brooklyn by the time he came to visit me.

I was trying to get to know Wayne. Finally, we got to talking and he gave me his telephone number. One day in December I invited him to go to *Handel's Messiah*. He said he would come and asked where it was. I remembered that while I was on the train going to see my cousins in the Bronx I had seen a sign for Hunter College, so I told him it was in the Bronx. Actually it was in Brooklyn. As it turned out, he went to the one in the Bronx and I went to the one in Brooklyn. I stood in the hallway waiting all the night. He never came. I called him the next day. He said he went to the one in the Bronx and never saw me. It was not until he got home that his mother asked, "Why didn't you try the other one in Brooklyn?" That was something we always laughed about, that I was there and he was someplace else for our first date.

It was January when Wayne came to Brooklyn to visit me. I was planning to move back to Boston to take training to work as a physician's office assistant when my friend's grandmother asked, "You are going to go back to Boston and leave that nice young man?" That is when I started looking to see if there was the same course I could take in New York City. The class was late at night and I did not like to come home so late, and Wayne could not always meet me, so I dropped that class and took a Hebrew class. The class was at Wayne's former high school. I would walk around and stand in places where I thought he used to stand when he was a young student. I still remember Wayne standing in the hall when he came to pick me up. He was so young and handsome.

I met Wayne is summer 1970, and earlier in spring 1970 I attended an Adventist convention that was in Atlantic City where I met Brother Roden and Perry Jones.[13] Perry said, "Here's Brother Roden." I was in awe of meeting the prophet whose booklets I had been reading.

I also met a Seventh-day Adventist girl on the bus on the way to the convention in Atlantic City. She was very religious and sold Seventh-day Adventist books. She said she was getting an apartment in St. Albans and that she needed a roommate. It had two bedrooms, so I moved in a few months later and helped her pay the rent. Now I was only twenty minutes away from Wayne's house. I was able to go to Wayne's house more and get to know his family. Within a year and a half we were married. Wayne finished college that same year.

MARRIAGE AND LIVING IN CAMBRIDGE, MASSACHUSETTS

With the wedding and Wayne's college graduation and Wayne's birthday in June 1972, we had a very big June.

After Wayne finished college he said he was going to get his Master's Degree in Library Science. When he told people this, they would look at him and say, "You're going to go to college to be a librarian? Why do you need to go to college for that?" Wayne said to me, "They think all you need to do is walk up, say you need a book and the librarian walks over and gives it to you. How did she learn how to do all that?" He earned his Master's Degree in Library Science at Columbia University. It was supposed to be a two-year program, but he did it in one year. We lived that year with his parents in a downstairs apartment. That was also the year I was pregnant with little Wayne.

After Wayne finished his year at Columbia he decided to attend Harvard Law School. We lived in student housing in Cambridge. Wayne's brother was also in Boston attending Tufts University. Little Wayne was six months old. My mother still lived in Boston with my brothers and sisters. If I had known I would live away from my mother from then on, I would have spent more time with her.

Every holiday we would run off to New York City. I was vegetarian and Wayne's family wasn't. They did not have pork, but they had clean meats. My husband ate meat. My daughter Anita said many years later that as a child she never understood why, but she could tell something was different: we were always eating at a different table. She said that if the children wanted certain things to eat, they would be told to ask if their mother wanted them to have it. She did not understand why she could not just eat the things she wanted, since she saw other family members eating as they wanted to.

Family Religious Differences

During these years, Wayne had his conflicts about different things. I was trying to keep him in the Adventist church, but there were some things he did not like about it. I tried to teach him the things I believed in as a Branch Davidian. When the Branch Davidians started taking the Emblems— the juice and cracker—twice a day as taught by Ben Roden, I sent the Emblems with the kids to school. He really was a patient man.

While we were living in the married student housing in Cambridge, there was a room that people used for functions. Once a month on the new moon day, I rented that room for about $20 for the day. We would have Branch Davidians come from New Bedford, Massachusetts, and New Hampshire. Sidney, a young man who was a nephew of John Ramsey, was helping the people in New Bedford. We learned more about the Branch message from him. Sidney said Branch Davidians were going to start a new thing that Passover; Branch Davidians were going to start having the Emblems every day at 9:00 a.m. and 3:00 p.m. That was really something different for us. Little by little, we got used to it. Every day at 9:00 and 3:00 we stopped whatever we were doing to have the Emblems. I did not work so it was easier for me. The kids were home by a certain time and they were still young, so it worked out for me to help them learn the truth. I didn't work outside the home for twenty-eight years. After I started working in 2000, though, I realized that these things were a conflict with work.

At 9:00 a.m. and 3:00 p.m. we stopped whatever we were doing for the Emblems. For an hour we had a Bible study. Eventually foot washing was added to it. The Seventh-day Adventist Church would have them only four times a year. The Branch Davidians started having them every day. Adventists said that was too many times. We answered that the scripture says "often," so why can't it be every day?

When the Emblems were served we did not need a priest. We were the priests in our own homes. That is the way it was in the early years of Christianity before there were ministers. At Passover, the lamb was slaughtered and they would have other people come in. In your home you are the priest.

The Emblems are grape juice and the cracker. We made enough whole wheat crackers for the week. When we were living in the Palestine camp,[14] we would flatten the dough into circles and then put them on the fire. We had no way to cook them but on an open fire and we put a grate over the fire pit. Novellette Sinclair[15] would turn them over on one side, then turn them over again. I can still see her flipping them. They were good, like pita bread.

When Wayne and I went to Adventist camp meetings, Wayne would say to the Adventists, "My wife has a different belief. Do you think you want to hear what she has to say?" Many people did. He kept hoping that I would be told by someone that I was wrong. He brought people to me. The Branch Davidians who met Wayne said he was a good candidate to become a Branch Davidian, although they were surprised that I had married him and not a Branch person. They believed that at some point he could become a Branch Davidian and that God had brought him into my life.

A GROWING FAMILY AND RELOCATING TO NEW YORK CITY

Anita was born in Boston in 1974 in the same hospital where I was born, Brigham and Women's Hospital. It was a special blessing to give birth to her at the same place. I was in a room with a Mexican lady and one day they brought Anita to her and her baby to me. I said, "This is not my baby." The lady looked over and said something in Spanish. Apparently our babies looked similar. Anita was a beautiful baby, and very intelligent also.

Wayne graduated from Harvard with his law degree in 1977. We were looking forward to the next chapter in our lives when I realized I was pregnant. We were going back to New York City. We moved to the apartment on the top floor of Wayne's parents' house. Anita was about to turn three years old, little Wayne was probably four and a half, and I was pregnant with Sheila.

Wayne went to work as a librarian at Yeshiva University. He would get the Jewish holidays off, so I would ask him to take us to the zoo and different places. He said, "Just because I have these days off, don't think this means anything!"[16] He stopped work maybe at noon or 3:00 p.m. for the Sabbath.[17] He wanted me to know that he was not drawing closer to anything I believed. I still think that it was not by chance that he ended up at that university.

MOVING TO NORTH CAROLINA

That summer while I was still pregnant with Sheila, Wayne said he had a job interview in Canada. Wayne and I left Anita and little Wayne with the aunts, and we went up to Canada for the interview. Wayne got the job a few months later. He told me the people he had seen in Canada gave him a job in North Carolina. I remember that when he first told me a pain went through my heart. Going south . . . I was really very nervous about the whole thing. Also, I thought of not being able to live in New York City where the children could grow up with their grandparents and being close to all of their other family members. Plus the Branch believers I knew were close by.

All of Wayne's schooling and jobs kept us moving back and forth between Boston and New York City. Now we were really moving away. It was only eight hours away, but we were not going to be able to get back north for holidays and other things with our families as easily as before.

I wanted Wayne to get better jobs and be successful. That meant going to where the jobs were. We moved to Durham, North Carolina, in June. Wayne became assistant professor and law librarian at North Carolina Central University. Sheila was just five months old. Anita and little Wayne were probably three and a half, and five years old. We went there with a little boy, a little girl, and a new baby.

We were scared. We had heard so many things about the South that we did not know what it would be like, but it worked out fine. Wayne enjoyed his time at the university. We were meeting people at church and our children were making friends. The Adventist church was nice. Things were going well. We were happy. The grandparents would come down on different holidays.

In 1979 I became pregnant with Lisa Marie, our third daughter and fourth child. Lisa was born at the Durham County General Hospital in January 1980. This was a very special pregnancy. I had an early miscarriage and I went to be examined by the doctor. I was given medicine to take for a week and told to return in a month. When I returned I was told I still showed being pregnant. An ultrasound confirmed it and the doctor was dumb-founded. The ultrasound showed it was a five weeks pregnancy. We continued the pregnancy. Lisa was a beautiful baby.

Wayne was still trying to find out why I believed the things I did. Even though in North Carolina I was not around any Branch Davidians to talk with on a daily basis, I still held to Branch Davidian beliefs and practices. We still had a connection to the Adventist faith. At some point, a letter and an audiotape were sent to our home from Mount Carmel. The letter and tape had to do with a meeting that they were having at Mount Carmel. I did not know what was going on, but there was a lot of discussion of things I knew nothing about. George Roden was complaining about something.[18] I think God kept me from hearing all these rumors so that I could focus on the truth. I was reading the Bible and trying to raise my children. In 1983 I received a letter saying that we were supposed to go to Mount Carmel to meet David.[19] I wasn't able to go at that time.

JAMIE BECOMES ILL: WAYNE BECOMES A BRANCH DAVIDIAN

Jamie—James Desmond Charles Martin—was born on May 31, 1982, in the Durham County General Hospital. I wanted so very much for Wayne to have a son in June. But I realized we missed it by one day even though it was the sign and character, not the date of the month, that I really wanted. I arrived at the hospital ready to have him a week earlier than the planned C-section date.

Jamie was a healthy, alert baby. We had a good summer with him, but during a visit to Washington, D.C. in September he began to show a different type of behavior. A few weeks later he began to cry as he did in Washington. By the end of the day he appeared to be fine, but over the next few weeks things deteriorated, and he was eventually diagnosed with bacterial meningitis.

In the Intensive Care Unit we saw people who were sad, waiting to see their loved ones. They were allowed only fifteen minutes each hour. That's all it was, fifteen minutes. You could get into ICU to visit the patient for fifteen minutes, then you had to wait forty-five minutes before being allowed in again. If someone else went in you might lose a whole hour or two before you got back in there. So many people were just sitting, waiting to get into ICU. It made me aware that when I was at home before Jamie got sick, watching TV, enjoying my life, these people were going through so much pain. Their moments each day had been different from mine. It was life and death for them, and now it was for me, too.

The Adventist minister came and put ointment on Jamie and prayed. The minister couldn't get the bottle open. I thought, "Oh, this is not going to work. He should be able to open the bottle, put the oil on him and pray, but he can't get the oil out the bottle." It took him a long time before he opened it. I thought, "Oh no, it should have worked better than this." I was thinking that God was not going to heal Jamie.

While Jamie was in the hospital, I remember going into the chapel and praying for a long time. I didn't want to leave the hospital. If Jamie was going to die I wanted everything to be there, even the funeral. I didn't want to go outside of that place of security. I didn't want to see him in a grave. I didn't want to see any of the things associated with the final goodbye. I prayed fervently for the Holy Spirit to come. I then felt I was being comforted. I was not alone. I needed to remember: "God answers prayers."

I remember another one of my prayers. I was visiting Jamie in the hospital. It was Halloween and the nurses were dressed up like witches and other Halloween characters. When the nurse came in I said, "Don't come," because I didn't want a witch there. I wanted good spirits around. As I was going out I leaned on the door and prayed, "Lord, please don't let him die today. I don't want him to die on Halloween. I don't want to think of him dead on every Halloween."[20] The next morning, I woke up and called the hospital to see how he was doing. They said, "He's doing fine. He's taking formula." They weren't going to feed him unless they thought he was going to live. I said thank you and hung the phone up and thought, "Oh no! Oh Lord, please, I know I asked you to let him die after Halloween but please let him live." I was so ecstatic. I needed to remember that God answers prayers, even though the doctors didn't think that Jamie had a chance of living.

We were in the hospital for five weeks. One day when they didn't have much hope for Jamie, I picked up one of Sister White's books[21]—*Counsels on Health*. I decided to read about preparing for death if Jamie was about to die. And then in my mind I heard: "Why don't you read about life instead?" I started reading all the things about God's ability to heal our bodies and souls. I read, thankfully: If you are allowed to drink the cup of woe, of disappointment, remember it's a loving God who is holding the cup to your lips. I have tried to remember that all through these past years.

Then the whole thing just turned. I started being encouraged and I continued to be encouraged. My husband could only see this little boy who was never going to run or talk. I just kept seeing, he's alive. God could do any miracle he wanted if he chose to.

After Jamie was taken out of the Intensive Care Unit, they told me I could hold him. I was in the room by myself. Wayne was back home with the children. I remember Jamie smiling at me. I put his toy keys in his left hand. He was shaking them and smiling at me. I thought, "I wish I had brought the nurse or the doctor in." I wanted them to see Jamie smiling. After the shunt operation it was eight months before he smiled again.

I remember the day they were going to give Jamie a shunt. I had left the house to stay with Jamie that night. Wayne had asked, "Can't you come home?" I went home and later I was told that Jamie had some kind of swelling in his brain that night. They had to rush to keep him alive by draining fluid from his brain. Wayne never asked me to stay home after that. He figured I was supposed to stay there and be close to the baby, that maybe my spirit was keeping him strong.

One of the men who came to fix the machines came over to where Jamie was lying. He looked at Jamie and said, "Boy, we could have put some money on this one, huh?" I was sitting there feeling that was a horrible thing to say in front of the mother. Maybe he didn't mean it as callously as it sounded: he was just trying to say he wouldn't have thought Jamie would come through it.

I spoke to Sister Roden and David by telephone while Jamie was in the hospital and after we brought Jamie home. After Jamie was out of the hospital Sister Roden told me that fresh juices were the best things for him. David prayed for us and Jamie. I felt a warmth when I spoke with David.

Jamie was not the same baby we went to the hospital with five weeks earlier. His disease was healed but he was left blind and greatly handicapped. His hearing was good, so we tried to keep music in his life at all times. He cried a lot and when I remembered the happy baby boy we came home with in May I felt the pain of his crying tenfold.

Jamie was my second son. I had wanted little Wayne to have a brother so very much after having three sisters in a row. Little Wayne was about nine years old when Jamie was born. I realized there was an age difference, but thought of how many brothers grow up to be great friends despite difference in their ages. But there were only a few months to think of their being brothers playing games together. My dreams were truly shattered. My hope in God was truly tested.

We began a new part of our lives, going to hospitals for years, and going to so many meetings about Jamie's health and progress, or lack of it. The fact that Jamie became sick was a shock to me. I was convinced nothing could go wrong. I realize now that my faith had to be tested.

As a result of Jamie's getting sick my husband started thinking about his religious beliefs. Wayne had been away from the Seventh-day Adventist Church for about three years. Then in the hospital, he read his Bible. He wasn't ready to go back to the church right away, because he said everyone was going to say that God had to touch the child to get him back to church. About a year after Jamie got sick in 1982, a young minister, who had encouraged Wayne to come to a meeting one night, called Wayne down to the front of the church. Wayne went down and was baptized again.

Through all of this David was on the phone whenever I'd call him. From the first time I spoke with David, he was there all the time. He let me call him at 6:30 in the morning and we'd talk for a short time. I didn't think Wayne would approve. Later Wayne said he was very glad I spoke with David during this time.

From 1982 to 1984 I spoke to the people at Mount Carmel by telephone. In January of 1984 a tape came to our home from David. Wayne came in from church one day when I had the tape on, because I had stayed home with Jamie that morning. I was going to turn the tape off, but Wayne said it was okay to finish listening to it. When the tape stopped I was going to turn it off, but he said, "No, turn it over and listen to the rest." I did not know if he was really listening. Later that evening, I noticed that Wayne was listening to the tape. He was picking up the Bible and reading the passages relating to what David said on his tape. He had never shown this interest before.

Wayne later said that it was important that he had a chance to read these things in the Bible for himself, and not just listen to David. He could stop the tape. He could study the Bible, think about it, and he said that is what made the difference.

Wayne listened to David's tape in January 1984. Two months later, David sent a note saying that people needed to come to Mount Carmel for Passover. My mother came and stayed with Wayne and the children while Jamie and I went on the plane to travel to Mount Carmel. Jamie and I stayed at Mount Carmel for a week.

When Jamie and I came to Mount Carmel in 1984 David was very patient with me. Jamie just cried and cried and cried.

Through all that crying, David told me to stay in the meeting, listen to the lesson, and not to leave the room. Once or twice I did go out with Jamie. People were looking at me because of the crying. But through it all David was continually holding Jamie. He'd pick Jamie up and hold him. David would go get him. He said, "You guys need more healing than Jamie." After we moved to Texas we never saw David being any other way than nice to Jamie, taking care of him, holding him, helping him into the bus to go to school. David was always telling us to show love and respect for that little boy.

After my visit to Mount Carmel in spring 1984, we got a visit in Durham from David and Novellette Sinclair in August. David was visiting Branch Davidians across the East Coast who came to Mount Carmel at Passover. Wayne asked David, "What if I do not accept this message?" David said, very quietly and calmly, "You'd be lost." Wayne said he never forgot how David said it. Perhaps Wayne expected him to rant and rave, but David was very calm and serious. Wayne was impressed by what David said and by his singing. When David played his guitar and sang all the kids went to sleep. All the people who were in that room, except for me, are gone now.

Later on in December of 1984 David said to some of the Branch Davidians I knew from Massachusetts, "Tell Sheila to come. We've had a lot of studies. She's missing out on all the things you're learning." When the time came, I said to Wayne, "You know, David was hoping we would come to Passover in '85," and Wayne said, okay. I went back to Wayne a few hours later and said, "I think he wants us to come there to live." Finally in April of 1985, Wayne said, "I want to go. I want to go and see what Passover is all about."

So that's how we joined the Branch Davidian community in Texas. It was Wayne's interest that took us there. After we visited the community for Passover, Wayne made up his mind to leave his job. We were going to get a bus, drive to the camp at Palestine, and live there. Everyone was supposed to get a bus and come out. We were going to travel all around the country, preaching, and talking to people, telling them all about the message.[22] That was the whole goal.

JOINING THE BRANCH DAVIDIAN COMMUNITY: LIFE AT THE PALESTINE CAMP

We visited the group in Texas in April of 1985 for Passover, leaving at midnight with Branch Davidian men driving their motorcycles before us and many families following in vehicles behind them. We arrived about 2:00 a.m. at the campground in Mexia, Texas, where David and the Branch Davidians from Mount Carmel were staying. We stayed for a week listening to many Bible studies from David, and then we left to go back to North Carolina to buy a yellow school bus and pack up our home. The bus was to be our new home on the twenty acres of property that David had purchased in the woods outside Palestine, Texas.

Wayne told his parents and my mother about our plans. They all said: It is one thing to move to another state and have a job. Now you are just going to move to another state and live in the woods! You don't know these people. But Wayne was determined. He knew he was ready.

When we left on a Thursday night, it was late and very dark. A thunderstorm caught us along the way. We were very scared and, because we were leaving everything behind us that we knew, it made me think of going back.

Wayne and I knew that when we got to Texas, we were going to see people who wanted to know about God and believed in the truth. We would have a chance to study together and make plans to travel to see the people in the country and the world. We were going to learn about the Bible to tell them about the kingdom that was coming. That was our goal. That is what we decided was the most important thing. We desired, also, a better and closer walk with God. We wanted our children to know God better. After thirteen years of having struggled to be one couple, to believe in the same truths, we were finally at the point where we were going to learn and study together.

We arrived at the Palestine camp on the fifth of May. We arrived just in time to get ready for the Sabbath. I was reminded of a statement that Sister White had made. She saw people leaving the cities and congregating in small towns. I thought, "My goodness, we have done that. We have left the cities. We have come to be in a small town." The thought that we were fulfilling a prophecy we had been reading about for so many years was exciting. We did not know exactly what it all meant, but we believed that David was going to lead us and tell us the right things to believe, and we would understand what needed to be done. We would get through. We would still be able to see our family members, and things would work out. We were not afraid.

We were happy to see the people at the camp. They were all trying to encourage us. They had lived together for quite a few years. They were in a new experience, also, by moving away from Mount Carmel. They did not know exactly what to expect, but they also believed that David would bring them to the right understanding of things.

We were getting up, having breakfast, sitting around a campfire, talking to fellow believers, and having Bible studies. The main thing David wanted us to know was that we had to get rid of all of the clothes, appliances, and other things that we did not need. We needed to start really believing that we were going to go to a kingdom, that God was going to start a new life for us one day. We had to be thinking better thoughts, changing all of our ways, and trying to put behind us the life we had known before we came to Palestine. We needed to let the Bible be first. We did not have a television. There was no electricity; we used candles or little lanterns. Little by little, the longer we stayed, the more we were able to fashion a life that provided showers and a kitchen.

We were able to keep the Sabbath and do the things we needed to do, but, of course, they were done all outdoors. We went inside the bus to go to sleep, but the rest of our living space was the whole twenty acres of land. We did not have to worry about furniture and clothes. We were slowly trying to get rid of all of the things we thought we had needed in our lives outside of the Palestine camp. We went to Wal-Mart, food stores, and did laundry at the washeteria, so much of the lifestyle was what we were used to doing, just a little bit inconvenient at times.

One precious memory I have is of Wayne and me sitting outside the washeteria waiting for the clothes to finish. We were watching the people inside interact. He turned to me and I realized he was watching me. He finally said he was very happy to have me for his wife.

Our days in Palestine were about studying our Bibles, getting our meals, taking walks, studying with David, and listening to his music. Some women were having babies. David would come back from his trips to California, and he brought his music equipment and a generator.[23]

By November of 1985 some of the people were on their way to California to work and spread the message. Wayne was one of those who left to go with David and some of the other men. Only a few months after the time we thought we would have a chance to learn together and share the truths together, Wayne and I were being separated. Wayne was beginning to learn some of the statutes of faith that I had been learning in all my years of growing up in truth. Wayne knew that he could go off to California and leave me and the children and everything would be fine. Knowing the truth was the most important thing that he wanted. He wanted very much to be able to learn the things that he had heard me talk about for so long, such as the kingdom and the 144,000 on Mount Zion.

Many of the people living in the Palestine camp were still working at their old jobs. Some were consultants and were able to fly back and forth. Others had jobs they would drive back and forth to. Some were able to return each night for Bible study and dinner with the families. There were always people finding some way to earn money.[24] Some people just gave up their jobs completely. Some people were able to go on food stamps. Family members also sent money and gifts.

Each family had to pay only $35 a month for food. They might pay more as they were impressed to do so. Of course, we did not have to pay any rent. At that time our family consisted of seven people. We thought that paying $35 a month for food compared to a $100 or more per week was a bargain.

I think Wayne was glad for that. We were able to tell the grandparents and other relatives that things were good.

I became pregnant with Daniel just before Wayne went off to California in 1985. We went up to New York City in 1986 for his birth. We stayed in New York five weeks. I thought because of the electricity and running water it would be more comfortable in New York City, but it was very hot there. It was not as hot at Palestine, because at the camp we had all the trees. We came back to Palestine in August and we were all glad to be back.

Before we left for New York City I remember David saying to me that it was not a place to go and put my feet up and drink lemonade. He was trying to tell me that leaving the group for a time was a serious situation. It was kind of similar to that night in Boston when John Ramsey and Nina came to me and said, you are getting ready to go to a school, and don't forget what you are here for and why. You do not want to give up truth. Before David told me not to look for the easy life at the grandparents' house, I had thought of doing just that: I imagined myself sitting there with my feet up drinking lemonade with ice. When David said those words to me I knew that God knew what I was thinking about. I had not told anyone my wish. That's how I knew it was of God that David knew what I was planning.

One time, Novellette Sinclair was able to get some ice without charge. We started taking our lemons and the honey that we usually had in our buses and we made drinks. David came back one day from California, and saw us sitting in our lawn chairs under the trees with our feet up drinking our lemonade and ice. When he saw us in this relaxed position, he said: You know, we're getting an army for God together.

Armies do not sit with lemonade under the trees relaxing. They're supposed to be ready at a moment's notice. We recognized then that God was trying to get us to realize that no matter where we came from in our earlier lives, our whole thinking had to be very different now.

David was always pointing out to us our mission for life. He seemed to know what was going on about things we had not told anyone.

Another one of my experiences with David's ability to receive God's messages came after I went up to Tyler, Texas, with my husband, to an iridologist who was going to be able to read Jamie's eyes. She also had a health food store. There were some chocolate chip cookies that I bought to give a piece to the children to get them up in the mornings. One night it was kind of late when we finished our meeting. David said, "Do you think any stores are open?" This was before there were twenty-four hour stores like Wal-Mart. He said, "I need to go to the store." So everyone was wondering, "What is he going to the store so late for?" The next day he gave everyone cookies. As soon as he said the word, "cookies," I thought, "Oh my goodness, this has something to do with me, I bet." He just kept giving out cookies and talking about different things. Everyone thought, "Someone has cookies. Somebody is eating something they are not supposed to be eating." That is why David did these things. Finally, he came into my bus and said, "I know there is something here," and the cookies were right near him. I did not know if I should say anything. I did not know what he was looking for because he did not say. Finally a day later I walked over and I said, "Did you buy those cookies because you think somebody else bought cookies?" He looked and said, "Oh, are you the one?" I told him I had bought some cookies and I went to get them to show him. David had a bottle of buttermilk in his hands. He saw that the cookies were the huge thick things that you put in the microwave. He said, "Here, you drink this milk with your cookies." He then sat down with me. Can you imagine what buttermilk tasted like with those microwave cookies? I ate one. I said something to him like, "Can I finish the other one tomorrow?" He said, "Oh no. Finish the whole thing. You must be really hungry." That night at the meeting he asked, "Are you ready?" I said, "Yes." He asked little Wayne, "Little Wayne, what did you think when your mother gave you those cookies?" My son said, "I guess she just wanted us to have a treat." David asked, "Didn't you think it was wrong to give you cookies to wake you up? How come you kids did not get up out of the bed when your mother said to get up?" Big Wayne later told me, "Sometimes I don't want to wake up either." It was not just the kids who had a problem with waking up in the morning.

I look back on all of these experiences and know that we went through them for a reason. God had a purpose for all of these things. Hopefully I've learned the lessons.

By 1987 more people were coming to join the group, especially from Hawaii. Around November the shootout with George Roden happened at Mount Carmel.[25] The sheriff's deputies came and arrested David and some of the other men. I remember I did not know anything about it until Lorraine Sylvia told me about it.[26] She said something had happened. She was not able to tell me much. We found out that some of our men were at Mount Carmel and George said he was shot at. David and eight other men were arrested. David's mother, Bonnie Haldeman,[27] bailed him out early. David said that in jail he was just about to go to sleep and rest. He said he had been dealing with people for two and a half years. Actually it was longer—since '83, with the people at Mount Carmel, before going to Palestine. He was saying he would probably be able to get a nice little rest in jail. When David and Paul Fatta were bailed out of jail,[28] they were not able to come back to Palestine. They had to stay in Waco.

We went over to Waco to visit them, I think in December, because it was a day when it was very snowy and icy. We went in the shuttle bus that they used to drive people back and forth to California. As we rolled down the road to Waco there was this quiet beauty of all the ice on the trees. Closer to Waco it was getting warmer. We already thought we were in a different world. In less than two hours we were arriving in another city, a big city at that, compared to the small town of Palestine. We stayed there one night. We had Bible studies with David, then the next day we went back to Palestine.

When we went to visit David we stayed at an old nightclub on a rundown street. It had black paint on the windows and David called it the Cave. That place is not too far from where I am living now.

Back in the Palestine camp Perry Jones kept saying that one day we would go to Waco to live. We kept trying to understand. What did he mean we are going to Waco? While waiting in the Palestine camp to hear of the trial of David and the other men, one morning in the latter part of March or early April of 1988, Perry came in at the end of our worship hour and said we were all supposed to get ready as quickly as we could to move to Mount Carmel.[29] We were stunned.

By the time we got this, that, and the other thing ready and put them all in the bus, we did not get to Mount Carmel until after 6:00 p.m. The reporters were waiting for us when we arrived. The news report showed us getting off the bus and going into Mount Carmel. David was in Waco. We stayed at Mount Carmel that first night, but then we learned that David did not want the women and children to stay there until the houses were cleaned and fixed up. So we went over to Kathy Jones' house,[30] which was a couple of miles from there. It turned out that certain people were allowed to go back over to Mount Carmel to help clean up and work. There was a phone at Mount Carmel, so I called up and asked for Larry.[31] I asked, "What is it like there?" She said, "Don't expect to have a hairdo! It is very windy!"

The wind came at Mount Carmel when we needed it. It kept us cool and lessened the burden of the heat, unlike being in the city with the hot streets. And we had the lake at Mount Carmel. The men would swim in it and there was fishing. There were beautiful sunsets every night. The sunsets were the first thing I noticed and I asked some of the Branch Davidians who had lived at Mount Carmel, "Why didn't you tell us about the sunsets?" I guess they had gotten used to them year after year. When you see it for the first time, it is quite an experience seeing such a big sun in such a big sky.

LIFE AT MOUNT CARMEL

Wayne and I had six children who came with us to Mount Carmel. Not long after we got to Mount Carmel in 1988 I became pregnant. Two other women and I were pregnant at the same time. These babies were being born not too far apart from each other. Kimberly became our seventh child in 1989. Wayne was amazed at how many other children were born at the same time our children were born and how close they were, like brothers and sisters. He believed that God was allowing so many children to be there so they could all be friends. Ofelia Santoyo's granddaughters[32] were friends with Lisa and Sheila.

We were waiting, to see what God was going to do, what he had planned for us, and how we were going to live one day in Israel. We were trying to get passports so we'd be ready when God told David it was time to leave America.[33]

New Light Message Changes Marriage Relationships

After a while things started changing again. In October of 1989, one day David came back from California and said he had a "new light" message to share with us: Did we really believe that the husbands and wives we had were the ones that God intended for us to be with? Or did we choose them ourselves? Do we really show love, or do we mostly hate each other? If we had a chance to live by ourselves again, how would husbands and wives treat each other? He said, maybe you husbands and wives do not really love each other, you just love parts of your bodies. He made us consider: What was it that God wanted? How were we relating to each other? Did God see us as being people of light? Were we people who truly understood what the disciples went through, what other people went through, the time and sacrifices they had made?

The single men had already been told that they were not going to be pursuing other women, that they should be changing their lives and dedicating them to God first. They were to be dedicated only to God, and waiting on God for another time to receive their wishes and desires.[34]

By October of 1989, David was telling us how God had mates for us in the kingdom; people who were truly a part of us were the mates we would be with. We should not want to have the mates that we were with now. There is a scripture in the Bible that talks about how at some point the people are going to mourn apart from their mates (see Zechariah 12:12-14). Clive Doyle said at that time, either they did not want their mates because they did not like them anymore, or God had shown them that these mates were not meant for them. He said you could take the meaning in two ways.[35]

We understood that we were to be more dedicated to God. The Catholics have the concept of believing in God, saving yourself for God only, being dedicated to God as priests and nuns. David said that was the ideal of what we were supposed to do, how we were supposed to conduct our lives, trying to do the right things and being more dedicated to God than to ourselves. He said that we did not love God. We thought we did, but we really did not. We love ourselves more than God. All we had to do was look at the way we lived and how we cheated one another from the love we should have given to each other.[36]

It was rough hearing this. Sometimes we laughed. Sometimes we were very quiet. Sometimes we put our heads down. He said, either way, he knew that we were listening and as long as we were there to hear what he said, he could help us. We were able to be strong with God.

David's Children

This was part of the situation in October of 1989 when David began explaining to us about our relationship to God. We had already noticed that there were a few children around who were not Rachel's children.[37] He started to explain to us that these were children that women had chosen to have with him, because they believed they were children from God.[38] He also explained that some of these children were people who had been in heaven. He said that they had made a choice to come down here to live, and to die, if necessary. They wanted to be a part of the experience.

Building a Spiritual Community

We were realizing that just because something was written down a certain way in the Bible—and people had told us for years it had a certain meaning—it did not mean that was the end of it. There was more meaning and more understanding to be gained. Sister White was always talking about how God had more truth. She said there was more understanding to come, that we were not to feel that she was the last prophet. She said people did not want to go into anything they felt was going to turn them from where they were. People were afraid to step off and look at things because they wanted to stay on the path that they were on. They liked to go to church. They were happy with their quiet lives. It was like going to a party every week. Every Sabbath you get dressed up, get special food, and see all of your friends.

We started saying we needed many changes in our lives. I remember I had some dishes I used for Sabbath. Perry was saying we were all going to share things and put things together in one place.[39] I started thinking about how I had my own mind on what I was going to do and how I was going to do it. Now we were being told we were all going to become more one-minded. I was watching a movie just recently. I think it was *White Squall*,[40] and the characters were on a boat.

One person was singing. The captain of the boat asked: Why aren't the rest of you singing? He said that singing together meant that they were all in one mind, they were all in unity. I thought about David and how sometimes he would have us sing together. He would say, "I want everybody singing." Usually it was Christmas songs. He would say, "It makes you feel good, doesn't it?" That Spirit that comes over people, he said, is why you like Christmas. But Christmas has nothing to do with Christ.[41] We also experienced that unity when we would dance together to David's music. We would dance often. We had fun but everything was to be a lesson in God's wisdom.

We were constantly changing. In 1989 David truly was telling us that we were going to have to make a great sacrifice and step out of the mold of what we knew in the past.

During that same year, Wayne's father, his mother, and my mother, came to visit us for a weekend. They stayed at a motel in town. At that time we had a house at Mount Carmel, but it had no water or electricity inside.[42] We had an extension cord running from one of the other houses, which ran the washing machine, radio, and lights. Water for washing came from the pond at Mount Carmel. Drinking water was trucked in from the Beaver Lake community two miles away, because the well on Mount Carmel had dried up. The grandparents had a chance to meet David. David had Bible studies for them and he provided a lot of food for lunch. This was around the same time that the new light was being revealed. We couldn't share the new light with them, yet.

Kimberly Is Born

Kimberly was born in January 1989. We lived in the house that Bob and Janet Kendrick originally had for their family.

They had five children.[43] There was one little room there that was pink. I think at one time Kathy Jones also had that house, and she had given birth to one of her children in the pink room where Kimberly was born. I wanted a little girl. We had pink this, pink that, pink diapers. Jaydean Wendel had a baby due at the same time.[44] I thought that Jaydean was going to have her child first.

I went to the laundry with everyone on Sunday, January 8. I was sitting down for a long time. When I stood up something felt strange. I thought I needed to sit down and that I would not do laundry after all. I walked around a little bit and when we were getting ready to go home, I told Wayne I felt pains in my side. He said we should go to the hospital, but I said, no, no, I am going back to Mount Carmel. Mary Belle Jones[45] said she was going to help me have the baby, and Bonnie Haldeman was going to come help because she was going to nursing school. Mary Belle came and checked the timing of my contractions and the pains. She went to see Jaydean Wendel because she was having pains, and said she would be back. She came back a little while later and said nothing was happening with Jaydean babywise and that she did not think anything was going to happen with me that night. She went back up to stay with Jaydean.

About 10:00 p.m. I felt like I needed to go to the bathroom. I put my hand on the bathroom door and my water broke. All the other times I had my babies in hospitals. This would be the first time at home. I got a little scared and I came out of the bathroom. I said, "Wayne, go get Mary Belle. Tell her my water broke." She came back and we prayed together. I walked around a lot. Finally at some point after midnight I went back into the bedroom, and sat down on a pillow on the floor next to the bed. I was not in a lot of pain, but I could feel pressure. At some point, I just turned to my right and I made an "ughh" sound. Dana Okimoto[46] was there. She was training to be a midwife. She said, "I think she is ready." I could feel my body pushing. I was not in a lot of pain. Eventually Kimi's head was born. They were telling me, you have to keep going. I did not feel any more pressure. They said, you have to keep pushing for the rest of her to come out. I got a little more strength to push and she was born. The first thing Bonnie said to me was, "Wow, I thought you would be a screamer."

Through God's grace I was able to have babies easily. Because Anita was so large, the doctor said I had to have a C-section. I had a C-section with Sheila and then with Lisa and with Jamie. When I had Daniel I went into the hospital and they expected to give me another C-section. I was lying in the bed and telling them how I did not feel well. I felt things going down my back and because I did not have a baby naturally with the last four children, I thought I was having bowel problems. I did not realize he was actually moving down the birth canal. I was feeling all of these different things but I did not know exactly what was going on. Finally I spit up something and after that my stomach really started pushing. Whatever pain I had was gone. I decided I was just going to lie there until the nurses came to get me. They came in and I told them I felt pushing. They said, "Take a deep breath and hold it." I said, "I can't do that!" Finally they brought me into the delivery room. One nurse saw the baby's head was already there and said, "What are we going to do?" The doctor said, "Tell her to push." The doctors were concerned because it was my first natural birth after four C-sections.

When Dana went to tell David that Kimberly was born, David said he wanted me to go to the hospital and get checked out. We went to the hospital and they could not believe I had a baby so recently because I was wide awake. They wanted me to spend the night and send the baby home. I wanted to stay, but I did not know that David would have one of the ladies at Mount Carmel nurse Kimi, so I said, "No, I will go home." But I certainly wanted to stay there in that bed and be pampered a little. If I had spoken up David might have told me to stay, but someone said, "You already had the baby. Why stay? You might as well go home." I should have spoken to David and told him the doctor wanted me to stay. He would have said, bring the baby home, or he might have said, come home with the baby. At least I would have known it was his decision, not only mine. I would have felt much better.

Living in the Big House

In 1990, 1991, and 1992, we were all just trying to learn more about the kingdom and see how much better we could become as children of God. David said we should have love for others and get along with people, and treat them better than we treat ourselves. Those were the things he said he would like to know he had taught us, and then he could feel that his being here meant something.

We started tearing down the small houses and using the materials to build the one large house. We started moving into the big house in 1992.[47]

When we came in to the chapel to have our Bible studies David always wanted us to have our Bibles with us. He said that was the only way we were going to learn. We were not going to learn by having our Bibles in another part of the house. When we heard the music coming from the chapel we would go in.[48] The seating in the chapel had been transformed from pews to graduated seating. Some of us would have our blankets and pillows and sit down in the front. Others would sit higher up where it was a little warmer. David said, one day I am going to have you people from the top come down here, and those of you on the bottom will go up top. We liked it in front because we were closer to him. We liked having our blankets and pillows there. Sometimes we fell asleep, and sometimes he woke us up. He said he preferred for us to be awake, but either way we would hear what he said.

Our experiences with David and how he treated and talked to us were really quite interesting. He was very funny at times, and at other times very serious. At 6:00 in the morning I would leave the meeting and get Jamie ready for school. By that time everyone else was either getting their children ready to go to school, going to work, or having breakfast.

Postponed Visit with the Grandparents

In 1992 we were thinking that the grandparents were coming to visit again, but during August ATF agents were talking to the man who had sold David guns. David invited the agents to come over to inspect his weapons, but they did not come over.[49] My husband told his parents and my mother that they should wait a little bit before coming to visit. He was thinking that he was going to go some place in August and he did not want them to come when he might not be there. The grandparents then planned to come for a visit in the spring of 1993.

THE ATF RAID ON MOUNT CARMEL, FEBRUARY 28, 1993

By January of 1993 we all were in the big house. Maybe there was one small house way down at the end of the road going towards the barn that was still kept open.

One day in February 1993 a reporter from the *Waco Tribune-Herald* came to speak with David. He told David that he was doing an article on the Branch Davidians and it was going to come out soon. He did not say when it would be out. None of us thought anything bad would come from a newspaper article. The first article that appeared on Saturday, February 27, talked about David as the "sinful messiah." The newspaper said there was going to be a new installment each following day on what we were doing at Mount Carmel. Thursday's article was going to be on the families and our lifestyles. We were anxious to read it.[50]

Robert Rodriguez had come to church that Saturday morning.[51] David had planned to have him come to the Saturday morning meeting and only certain people were going to join them. He did not want Robert to be overwhelmed with too many people there. At 8:00 in the morning there was a knock on the door of my room. Rachel Howell said David wanted all of us to come down to the meeting. I said, "I thought some of us were supposed to stay." Rachel said, "Something has happened." When we got downstairs, there were a lot of newspapers on the table by David's chair. Robert Rodriguez was there. David was discussing the newspaper article and all the things he thought were going to happen. David said, I do not think they like us living here like this and they are probably going to make trouble. We had the Bible study and Robert left at 12:00. He said he would come back later that night.

Photo 1: Wayne Martin about 1972.

Photo 2: Sheila Martin with Anita and Lisa (7 months) in 1980.

Photo 3: Anita and little Wayne in the bathtub in 1977.

Photo 4: Lisa, Anita holding Jamie, Wayne, and Sheila, probably in 1984.

Photo 5: The four oldest Martin children about 1986 in the Palestine camp. Top row left to right: Anita and Wayne. Bottom row left to right: Lisa and Sheila.

Photo 6: Some of the children at the Palestine camp. Sheila and Lisa Martin are on the left, Rachel Sylvia is in the middle, the children of Floyd Houtman are on the right. Photo courtesy of Bonnie Haldeman.

Photo 7: Martin Family in 1987 at Wayne Martin's parents' home, visiting from Palestine, Texas. Back row left to right: Wayne Martin holding Jamie, Sheila Martin holding Daniel, young Wayne, Anita. Front row left to right: Lisa, young Sheila.

Photo 8: Wayne Martin and Greg Summers using a computer at a club called the Cave on 19th Street in Waco, where David Koresh's band used to practice. Photo courtesy of Bonnie Haldeman.

Photo 9: Photo taken on February 28, 1993, of the front of the residence. Sheila Martin's room is visible on the far right on the second floor. Bullet holes can be seen in the wall around Sheila's window, in the wall around the window next to Sheila's room, and in the double front doors. Defendents' exhibit in the 1994 criminal trial.

Photo 10: Tank entering the front doors to the Mount Carmel residence during the FBI tank and CS gas assault on April 19, 1993. The window to Sheila's room is on the far right, second floor. Government exhibit photo in the 2000 civil trial.

Photo 11: Photo taken on April 19, 1993, showing the fire starting in Sheila's room on the second-story front east end of the building. The Branch Davidian flag is visible just above the fire. Government exhibit in the 2000 civil trial.

Photo 12: After the building is completely burned down, a fire truck is permitted to spray water on the hot ashes. Government exhibit in the 2000 civil trial.

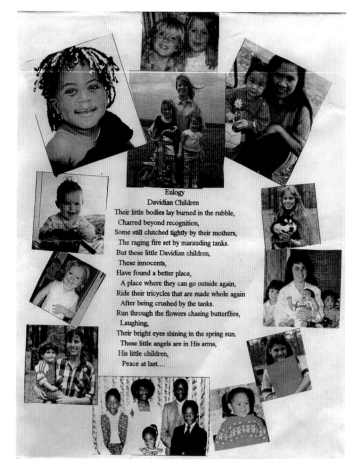

Photo 13: Collage of Branch Davidian children with poem entitled "Eulogy: Davidian Children." The children and their mothers from the top clockwise: Cyrus and Star Howell Koresh (ages 8 and 6 in 1993) (top photo); Rachel Howell Koresh and Cyrus and Star (all died in the fire); Floracita Sonobe (died in the fire) and Angelica or Crystal Sonobe (sent out during the siege); Shari Doyle (died in the fire); Jaydean Wendel (died in shootout with ATF) and Juanessa, Landon or Tamara, and Patron Wendel (sent out during the siege); Rachel Sylvia (died in the fire, 13 in 1993); Angelica or Crystal Sonobe (sent out during siege); members of the Henry family (died in the fire); Lorraine Sylvia (died in the fire) and Joshua Sylvia (sent out during siege); Cyrus Howell Koresh; Dayland Gent (died in the fire, age 3 in 1993); Melissa Morrison (died in the fire, 6 in 1993).

Mt . Carmel Center
April 19,1993, 1 yr.

We Can't Forget

Mellissa Morrison	6
Lisa Martin	13
Sheila Martin	15
Mayanah Schneider	2
Serenity Jones	4
Startle Summers	1
Bobbie L. Koresh	2
Star Howell	6
Cyrus Howell	8
Abigail Martinez	11
Audrey Martinez	13
Crystal Martinez	3
Isaiah Martinez	4
Joseph Martinez	8
Chica Jones	2
Little One Jones	2
Dayland Gent	3
Paiges Gent	1
Rachel Sylvia	12
Hollywood Sylvia	2
Chanel Andrade	1
Unborn child	
Unborn fetus	

Photo 14: Bookmark with the names of the children and their ages who died in the fire. Correct name spellings and ages: Melissa Morrison (6); Lisa Martin (13); Sheila Martin (15); Mayanah Schneider (2); Serenity Sea Jones (4); Startle Summers (1); Bobbie Lane Koresh (2); Star Howell (6); Cyrus Howell (8); Abigail Martinez (11); Audrey Martinez (13); Crystal Barrios (3); Isaiah Barrios (4); Joseph Martinez (8); Chica Jones and Little One Jones (twins, 2); Dayland Gent (3); Paige Gent (1); Rachel Sylvia (13); Hollywood Sylvia (2); Chanel Andrade (1); two unborn infants who died in the fire (their mothers were Nicole Gent and Aisha Gyarfas).

Photo 15: Sheila and Jamie Martin are reunited with Kimberly and Daniel Martin at the Dallas-Fort Worth International Airport in October 1993.

Photo 16: Daniel and Kimberly in 1994 holding a photograph of their father Wayne Martin.

Photo 17: *Daniel and Kimberly Martin in 1994.*

Photo 18: *Jamie Martin's funeral (coffin in far left corner) in 1998 at the pauper's field where his father and older siblings are buried. Sheila Martin embraces Daniel and Kimberly on the far right. Photo courtesy of Bonnie Haldeman.*

Photo 19: Kimberly Martin contemplates a faded funeral wreath that was donated to the Branch Davidians from someone else's funeral on the occasion of the February 28, 2003, memorial service marking the tenth anniversary of the ATF raid. The house used as the "undercover house" by ATF agents in 1993 is seen on the horizon, across the road, on the left.

Photo 20: Sheila Martin gives an interview to reporters on February 28, 2003, while standing among the crape myrtle trees at Mount Carmel. A crape myrtle tree was planted for each of the Branch Davidians who died in 1993.

MOUNT CARMEL CENTER

On February 28, 1993 a church and its members known as Branch Davidians came under attack by ATF and FBI agents. For 51 days the Davidians and their leader David Koresh stood proudly.

On April 19, 1993 the Davidians and their church were burned to the ground. 82 people perished during the siege. 18 were children 10 years old or younger.

ANDRADE, Jennifer	HENRY, Vanessa	GENT, Unborn Fetus	SAIPAIA, Rebecca
ANDRADE, Kathy	HENRY, Zilla	MALCOLM, Livingston	SCHNEIDER, Judith
ANDRADE, Chanel	HIPSMAN, Novellette	MARTIN, Anita Marie	SCHNEIDER, MAYANAH
BENNETT, Alrick George	HIPSMAN, Peter James	MARTIN, Douglas Wayne	SCHNEIDER, Steven
BENTA, Susan	HOLLMAN, Floyd	MARTIN, Lisa Marie	SCHROEDER, MICHAEL
BLAKE, Winston	HOWELL, Cyrus	MARTIN, Sheila Renee	SELLERS, Clifford
BORST, Mary Jean	HOWELL, Rachel Olivia Suzanne	MARTIN, Wayne	SONOBE, Floracita
COHEN, Pablo	HOWELL, Star	MARTIN, Diane	SONOBE, Scott Kojiro
DAVIES, Abedowalo	KORESH, Bobbie Lane	MARTINEZ, Abigail	SUMMERS, Aisha Gyarfas
DOYLE, Shari Eleysa	KORESH, David	MARTINEZ, Audrey Marlene	SUMMERS, Startle
ELLIOT, Beverly	JEWELL, Sherri Lynn	BARRIOS, Crystal	SUMMERS, Unborn Child
FAGAN, Doris	JONES, Chica	BARRIOS, Isaiah Taco	SUMMERS, Gregory Allen
FAGAN, Evette	JONES, Little One	MARTINEZ, Joseph Samuel	SYLVIA, Hollywood
FARRIS, Lisa Marie	THIBODEAU, Michelle	MARTINEZ, Juliette Santoyo	SYLVIA, Lorraine
FRIESEN, Raymond	JONES, Serenity Sea	McBEAN, John Mark Stanley	SYLVIA, Rachel
GENT, Peter	JONES, David Michael	MONDELLY, Alison Bernadette	VAEGA, Margarida
HARDIAL, Sandra	JONES, Perry Dale	MORRISON, Melissa	VAEGA, Neil
HENRY, Diana	LITTLE, Jeffrey	MORRISON, Rosemary	WENDELL, Jaydean
HENRY, Paulina	LITTLE, Nicole Elizabeth	MURRAY, Sonia	WENDELL, Mark W.
HENRY, Philip	GENT, Dayland Lord	NOBREGA, Theresa	
HENRY, Stephen	GENT, Paiget	RIDDLE, James Jude	

THIS MEMORIAL DONATED BY THE
NORTHEAST TEXAS REGIONAL MILITIA OF TEXARKANA, TEXAS
MAJOR DAN POWELL, COMMANDER

Photo 21: Memorial stone at Mount Carmel donated by the Northeast Texas Regional Militia of Texarkana, Texas, listing the names of all the Branch Davidians who died there in 1993. Photo taken on February 28, 2003.

Photo 22: The crape myrtle trees in bloom at Mount Carmel in August 2003. The house across the street that is most visible was the "undercover house" for ATF agents who were conducting surveillance before the February 28, 1993, ATF raid. When Catherine Wessinger visited in October 2004 the undercover house had been demolished.

Photo 23: Sheila Martin on April 19, 2003, at the paupers' graveyard in Waco, where her husband and five oldest children are buried, tells the account of how Marjorie Thomas stepped on her daughter Sheila as Marjorie was stumbling out of the burning building on April 19, 1993. Marjorie said, "Excuse me." Sheila said, "That's okay." Sheila Martin used this story to illustrate that the Branch Davidians were nice to each other even in the midst of the fire. Sociologist Stuart Wright is on the left.

Photo 24: Jamie Martin's grave in the paupers' field where he is buried with his father and older siblings. Photo taken on April 19, 2003.

Photo 25: Sheila Martin with Clive Doyle (left) and Catherine Matteson (right) speaking in the Mount Carmel chapel to scholars attending the CESNUR international conference on new religious movements hosted by the Baylor University's J. M. Dawson Institute for Church-State Studies, June 2004. Not shown is Bonnie Haldeman (far right), who was also on the panel.

Photo 26: Sheila and Kimberly Martin at Mount Carmel in August 2003. The chapel was built in 2000 on the site of the large residence that burned in 1993.

Photo 27: Martin family in 1990 or 1991. Back row L to R: Wayne
Joseph Martin, Douglas Wayne Martin holding Kimberly Reneé
Martin, Anita Marie Martin. Front row L to R: James (Jamie)
Martin, Daniel West Martin, Sheila Martin, Sheila Reneé Martin,
Lisa Marie Martin.

We continued our meeting. David said that he did not know if we would be together to have Passover in April. He said, I do not know what they are going to do. He was thinking about those men living across the street and Robert coming over. He thought Robert was an agent. He said, it looks like they are closing us down. Ruby Ridge had just happened.[52] That was the other reason that David was not sure what all of this was going to turn into. We came back later that night and we had music and a talent show. We did all of the things that were a normal part of the day and night. Robert left and David told us to be up early.

Early on Sunday morning, February 28, Robert Rodriguez was outside with Perry Jones and Catherine Matteson.[53] They were standing there looking at the newspaper and reading it. I went upstairs. When I came back down, Robert was in the hallway with David. I turned around and went back up the other stairway. I thought I shouldn't interrupt when David was talking with Robert. When Robert left, he went out to his truck to drive down the driveway and across the street where he and the other men were living. I heard a siren coming from his truck and then he beeped the horn four times. I went to the window and wondered, "Why did he do that?"[54] He had never beeped his horn when he left before. Why all the noise?[55]

After Robert left David told all of us ladies to come down to the chapel. While we were sitting there, Perry came in with David Jones and said they had just found out that there was going to be a raid. They said, the police are going to come. We thought maybe a car or two were coming. David thought maybe he would go downtown with them and it was not going to be too much of a situation. We accepted it and then I went back upstairs. I remember making sure little Daniel was dressed and I was telling him, "Daniel, I do not think we are going to live here after today." He said, "Why?" I said, "I do not know. I think something is going to change." I remember saying those words: "I do not think we are going to live here after today." Much earlier Bob Kendrick had said, "Don't think they are going to let us live here if they take David. Once David is gone they will be telling us we all have to leave."

We were upstairs in our room and Rachel Sylvia, Lisa's friend, came in and said, "Look out the window." She was thirteen, the same age as Lisa, and was Lorraine Sylvia's daughter. She let me know that there was someone outside. When I looked out, I saw one truck come up and stop and then I saw another truck come. The trailers pulled by the trucks were covered with tarps and I thought they contained wood.[56] My first thought was, "Wow, did we buy all of this wood?" I thought, "This is a lot of wood. I wonder what he is building this time." Before the second truck could stop, a man jumped out. He had a gun in his hand. I was still standing there looking, not thinking anything bad was going to happen. I was just watching what was going on. I heard some talking downstairs. The front door was underneath us to the right of my window. Then I heard a voice outside. Then I heard a voice inside. Then I heard a loud sound on the outside. The little girl, Rachel Sylvia, ran out of the room. I just knew to turn around and get the two children down. Then we started seeing all these shots come in the window. The shots were coming through the wall and the window. Jamie was screaming. Kimi and Daniel were saying, "What's happening?"

Jamie was on a couch in front of the window. I had put him there earlier to hear the birds. I had opened the blinds so he could see the light. With all the shooting I did not know how I was going to get him. I thought he was going to die over there. I thought, "Is this how he leaves me? Is this how he dies?" After all the years of taking care of him—he was ten and a half by then—is this how he leaves me? There was a lull in the shooting so I went over to get him. When I got over there I put my hand on his elbow to pull him down to the floor. Shots started coming in through the window again. I was crawling on my hands and knees to get him and come back, keeping as low as I could. He was screaming and I noticed his face had blood on it. I wiped his face. Something sharp, I guess the glass, had fallen on his face. Kimi and Daniel were lying on the floor asking me, "What's wrong with Jamie?" Daniel asked, "Why are the bad men here? Why are the bad men doing this?" I told him I did not know. I did not know what was wrong, what was going to happen.

There was a time when there was a man underneath the window. I heard him say, "Three men down, God damn it." Later they said four ATF agents died but he said he had three men down. So I do not know when the fourth one happened.[57]

When it was quiet, I went to the wall to the room next door and banged on it. I spoke to Larry. I asked, "Lorraine, what are we supposed to do? Are we supposed to just stay here? Are we supposed to go out of our rooms?" She said, "I do not know. I guess we are just supposed to stay here."

At one time while the shooting was going on, one of the people, I think it was Michele Jones,[58] crawled down the hallway asking me how I was. She said David wanted us not to be afraid, the children would finish the work. What he meant was that if the adults were killed, the children would continue the message.[59] I did not know that in her room, when the shooting started, her little baby tried to climb up on the bed. It was one of her twins. That is where she always nursed, so perhaps she figured her mom was up there. We could hear shots going through the walls, up through the floors.

After the shooting began I started hearing another noise in my husband's office on the first floor underneath my room. I could hear Wayne's voice shouting from underneath the boards of my floor. I could not hear what he was saying, but I kept hearing his voice. Later on I realized that he was on the phone, telling them to call it off, that there were women and children in Mount Carmel.[60] He was shouting from a place far away from the phone because of the gunshots coming in, and that was why he was so loud.

Much later in the evening my husband was able to come up and make sure that all of us were okay. I think his mother and father were the last ones to get through on the telephone line before it was cut off by federal agents to outside calls. Wayne said that he told his mother and father that we were fine and that we understood what all of this meant. I guess he was trying to say that if he had to die, that he would.[61] He said that all of us were ready for what was next, even death. They had not seen us for three and a half years, not since 1989. They were anxious to see us, and anxious to know what was happening.

When they started talking about the ceasefire, I heard a shot come from underneath me. One girl in the room above me later said she saw a bullet come through the floor. I began to wonder where I should put the children. I was thinking of putting the children underneath the bed. But then I thought that if the agents are underneath, they could shoot through the floors, so what were we going to do? We were stuck near some boxes of clothes and underneath the mattress trying to stay alive.

When they started saying things about a ceasefire, I loved it. I kept hearing "ceasefire," "ceasefire," everywhere. I was so glad that they were stopping. Someone came to my room and said that the agents were leaving. I did not want to look out. I was afraid to go to the window. Later when I was in jail, I saw on television the scenes of the agents going away from Mount Carmel. I didn't look out the window that day. I was afraid. I believed they would return with a vengeance.

THE SIEGE

On Sunday evening I heard that children were going to leave and they would let me know about Kimberly, Daniel, and Jamie. We were still scared, but stayed in our rooms trying to do the best we could in spite of all that was happening outside. We were trying to get food and function as normally as possible. There were many calls on the phone to the ATF. The agents said they were not going to do any more shooting. As long as we did not shoot, they were not going to shoot. Everyone felt happy about that. There was no one on our side trying to hurt anyone. We looked outside through a telescope and saw things happening up the road.

On Tuesday morning, March 2, Jamie and Joshua Sylvia, and later Daniel and Kimberly left. Jamie and Joshua went out at 2:00 in the morning. Jamie went to a home for the handicapped and Joshua went to the Methodist Children's Home. Catherine Matteson and Margaret Lawson went out later that morning with Daniel and Kimberly, and David sent an audiotape out with Catherine Matteson.[62]

It was dark when we brought Jamie out. I carried him and had my left hand against his head so he would not hit his head as we went out the door. My hand brushed against the metal of the front door and my finger was cut so deeply that the cut was still there when I went to jail three weeks later. The door's metal was jagged from the bullet holes in it.

David was the one who decided that the children would be sent out. He showed the FBI agents his good intentions by sending children out. Maybe at that point David was trying to see how things would go if he cooperated with the agents.

By 2:00 p.m. on that day I thought we were going to be leaving. The remaining children were going to go out first, then adults, then David, who was wounded, would be carried out. I was waiting downstairs, but no one came. I went upstairs and people were sitting down close to David praying. We stayed there until darkness. Then we started hearing loud rumbling sounds. David said, "It sounds like tanks coming. It would have been better for us to have died in the first shootout. Now they will shoot at us with tanks. We will see our legs and arms someplace and we will still be alive, dying a horrible death."

David and the others got back on the phone with the agents. David said that God told him to wait and that is what we did.

Then we started a new experience of living inside that place. The first night or so we had lights. At some point I had to go into my room to get something. It was dark in my room, but the light was on in the room next door. I looked at the wall where the kids and I were during the shootout. I saw that all above where our heads had been were gunshot holes. It looked like stars. You know how stars are sprinkled? The

ATF agents were determined when they were shooting at us. They knew that the women and children had rooms on the front side of the building on the second floor.

I didn't see agents in the helicopters shooting.[63] When the kids and I were in our room during the shooting, we saw a helicopter come from the side to the front of the building. We were on that side. But we did not see any shooting from the helicopters. We did not see anything like what Catherine Matteson said she saw on her side of the building.[64]

We went into a new life of going down to the kitchen, getting our food and water, watching the things outside, just trying to live day by day. The negotiators sent us video-tapes of the children who had been sent out. We watched them on the big-screen TV. We didn't know then where they were, and I asked myself, "What place here in Waco do I know that has all that brick?" Then I realized it was the Methodist Children's Home. We found out later that was where they were.

We sent some videotapes out.[65] Later the FBI agents said the reason they did not show those tapes on television was they thought people would say, look at these little kids, look what they (the agents) have done. They did not release those videotapes until long after everyone was dead, well past the summer.[66] I am getting ready to go and look at them again. I could not before. I could not look at the videotape called "Inside Mount Carmel." I could not bear to remember how beautiful they were. But I want to see it again. I want to see Lisa . . . to see if they are all there . . . I am not sure if I can watch it.

When agents sent their tanks, we started looking out and saw many things happening outside on our once beautiful grounds. I went upstairs once to the very top of the central tower. It might have been a week or two later. I did not see as many trucks and cars of spectators and news reporters as people said there were in the beginning of the siege.[67]

Eventually some of us made up our minds that we were going to leave when David said it was possible for us to go. It was about three weeks into the siege when we decided we were going to leave. David and Steve Schneider[68] made the arrangements with the FBI agents for us to leave. David asked me, "Are you ready for your journey?" I said, "I've been thinking about it." David said to all of us, when you go into the jail you can bring your Bibles. He said we would be out of jail soon because the FBI just wanted to talk to us. We believed the FBI agents would treat us with respect.

On March 20th Steve Schneider said it would be our last Sabbath together. He said we were all going to move off Mount Carmel a few at a time. Everyone was supposed to leave eventually. We were not going to all go at once in the buses like they wanted us to do. The FBI wanted us to look like we were all being marched down to the end of the road and put in buses and taken away like prisoners.

I went out on the 21st of March.[69] I believed I was coming back. I figured when my other children came out, Lisa and Sheila, who were thirteen and fifteen, were going to go to the Methodist Children's Home. I figured that Anita and Wayne, who were eighteen and twenty, were going to go to jail for a couple of days. I had no thought of "let me take these [older] children out" because many times they had said, "Mom, no matter what happens, if you want to leave, we want to stay. We just want you to know, just in case you start thinking about leaving." That was years earlier. We had been there five years or so. During that time they had come to know God and the scriptures for themselves. They knew where they wanted to be. So I had no thought, "Should I take them?" There was the feeling at Mount Carmel of what am I preparing for? What am I reading in the Bible? Are we all here together to be able to stand for truth and stand for the things we believe?

I believed that the kids were going to be in different places when they came out: the oldest kids would be in jail, the youngest ones in the Methodist Children's Home. When April 19 came it did not happen. They were gone.

EXPERIENCES AFTER COMING OUT OF MOUNT CARMEL

Going to Jail

It took a long time for the few of us who came out on March 21 to be processed. When we came out they handcuffed us, took us into that tank, and then into a car and over to the sheriff's office, where the FBI asked us questions about everything we had seen and was anyone sick. Eventually we got to the Texas State Technical College campus where we were finger-printed and had to put on orange jump suits. Then they drove us to the jail. It was getting dark when we passed that road where you see an overpass and you know you are going home to Mount Carmel. I looked down the road and thought, "I'm not going home tonight. Home is way over there." I felt like I didn't know whether I'd ever be back.

I didn't know that I had seen my husband and oldest children for the last time. I just assumed they were coming out. I remember my daughter Sheila had a pretty sweater on when I left and she had curled her hair up with her fingers. She looked so pretty. I'm just so thankful I have that memory. She picked out a red sweater for me to wear. Sheila said, "Wear this sweater. People are going to see you." We had such a strong spirit.

Anita was so much taller than Sheila. She was almost as tall as her dad. And my oldest son was taller than his dad. I remember that when Anita was born she was 9 pounds, 6 ounces. My husband looked and he said, "Can you promise me she's not going to get taller than me? Sure?" You can see in a couple of pictures she was getting tall. I was not so sure she wouldn't get taller than Wayne. She was shy when she was little, but when she was seventeen or eighteen years old I saw them being very close. I was so happy that she and her dad were actually having conversations with each other.

When Anita was a teenager, she was going to say something to me and I'd go, "Anita, don't do this." Then one day I decided I was going to change it around. When she came to me I said, "You're not being nice to me." Then she said, "Mom, stop that." And I said, "But you're going to make me cry." And she said, "Stop that. I am not going to make you cry. Stop it." It broke the ice. She didn't want me to look sad. I remember that, just now thinking about it, how we were beginning to have such a great relationship and plus she had moved up over my room to the third floor and the girls were up there, too. Lisa, Kimi, Daniel, Jamie, and I were all in the room on the second floor.[70] It sounds like a lot of people, but we really had enough room. It was a nice room.

I spoke with them the day I left thinking I was going to see them again. I was still in jail a week and a half later. I was wondering: "Where are they?" The jail had a whole section set aside for the ladies. I was wondering, "When are they coming?" They had us behind glass but we could watch the TV and see what was going on. Of course, by 10:00 p.m. we had to go to sleep, so I couldn't see everything on television, but I heard enough about what was happening to the property and what was said in the news conferences. Later when we went to the Salvation Army halfway house we saw the news every day.

On the first day when they took us to jail, I was standing at a desk with three other Branch Davidians when a guard came over and stood by me. First he looked at someone else, then another guard said, "No, this one," pointing at me. The guard took me away to a pink room. I asked, "What is this place?" It was all pink. There was nothing in there, only a hole in the floor. They put a mat on the floor much later. A guy next door was banging on the wall and screaming. I did not think this was where I was supposed to be, so I knocked on the door. Someone came and I said, "Byron Sage said if we need anything you're supposed to tell him and he will help us."[71] So they moved me into another place that had a window and a bathroom. I didn't know until later that they had cameras in there. I kept saying, "I need something to hold up to the window so I can go the bathroom." It was very cold and I was given a blanket. It was supposed to be a better place. I just cried the first couple of nights. I was thinking, "Oh my God. What's happening? What's going to happen?" I was trying to figure it out without the other believers there to talk to.

We were confident before we left that we didn't have to be afraid. We thought we would be able to leave jail in a couple of days. We hadn't done anything. They were going to keep us as material witnesses.

On Monday they sent me to take a lie detector test. They thought I knew things since I was Wayne's wife. Gladys Ottman asked for Mr. Coker, the lawyer David had used during the trial in 1988, and I asked for him, also. Mr. Coker came to talk to both of us, and he got me moved out of the place I was in to where the other Branch Davidian ladies were.

On Tuesday they let me go to the other cell to join the five women who came out with me on March 21st. We were all six of us in this little tiny place, with a couple of cots and the rest of us on the floor. The meals were good at first. They packed the plates with so much food we couldn't eat it all. The whole week they just kept bringing food and drinks. They were trying to do everything they could to make us feel good so we would answer their questions. When I joined the ladies in that room, I said, "Hey, I didn't know we were having a slumber party here!" Everyone was trying to be in good spirits, not realizing what was ahead.

When they took us upstairs to another part of the jail, we were saying, "I want this room," "I want that room." So the jailor came and said, "Ladies, please. I'm in charge." The FBI told them we were not regular prisoners; but then after Thursday they said, no one has come out. No more special food. One time I said, "It looks like ham is in the macaroni and cheese," so they sent it back. It took a long time for them to bring the food back. They stopped special treatment after people stopped coming out of Mount Carmel.

Some Branch Davidians were sent to the Salvation Army halfway house after a few days. Mr. Coker said they were trying to find a lawyer who lived close by to take me in. I asked,

"Are they going to let me bring the kids there, too?" They couldn't find a place for me, so I stayed a day later in jail than the rest. I remember walking back and forth, pacing in this holding place they had me in, because I was thinking, "I don't know if I want to go. I want to be here when all the rest of the people come out." It had been a week and a half and they still hadn't come. I could see their faces. I could feel them. I could imagine hearing their voices and talking to them.

Daniel and Kimberly were at the Methodist Children's Home. Wayne's parents were waiting until everyone came out so they could come and get all the kids at once and take them back to their house in New Jersey. That's why Daniel and Kimberly were still there at the Methodist home long after the time I thought they had left there.

The Salvation Army Halfway House

The Branch Davidian women who were let out of jail went to a halfway house. The government pays the Salvation Army money for the people who stay there. There were people there who were serving the last six months of their sentences. This halfway house was for men and women.

We were with everyone in the cafeteria and the common room. We even had to go to some Alcoholics Anonymous meetings, just because we were there. We were truly in a situation that we had never imagined.

The Branch Davidian women were in one room. We would get up early and pray and study.

Hoping to Get the Children

April 19th was on a Monday. The Friday before the fire I saw Jamie, Daniel, and Kimberly. While I was in the Salvation

Army halfway house I could leave with another person and go to see them once a week. Sometimes I took them to Wal-Mart to shop. While at the Wal-Mart on Friday, April 16, I saw a tabloid with all my children in it as we stood in line. I still have it.[72] It seems like an eternity has passed every time I look at it.

That weekend I thought, "Since I'm getting ready to come out of the Salvation Army halfway house, why don't I just ask for the children?" I thought, "On Monday I'm going to Child Protective Services and say that since I'm going to be able to leave the halfway house soon, I see no reason why Kimberly and Daniel and Jamie should leave Waco."

THE FIRE, APRIL 19, 1993

Monday morning came. At 6:00 a.m. I was in the cafeteria of the Salvation Army halfway house and I heard a guy talking about "window" and "tank." I wasn't paying attention because he was talking to one of the workers. Finally he looked at me and he said, "There are tanks at the window at Mount Carmel." I said, "What?" He said, "There are tanks at the window." I rushed into the television room, turned on the TV, and there it was—tanks backing out of the building. I said, "Oh my goodness." I went to tell the rest of the people. Anetta Richards, Catherine Matteson, Ofelia Santoyo, and Rita Riddle were there, and also a lady from Canada, Gladys Ottman.

I told them what was happening and ran back to the TV. They came and we were watching it and listening and silently praying. By 10:30 a.m. the FBI agents were talking at a press conference about what was going to happen, that the gas[73] was going in and that the people could not wash it off. I was hearing all these things they were saying, and in the back of my mind I was thinking, "It's over. I will see them all soon."

Before the special report came on the television at 10:30 a.m., law enforcement agents came to get Rita. They put her in shackles and took her off to jail. I think they felt Rita was a troublemaker. She had so much to say, and she was on the phone speaking to different reporters all during that time in the halfway house.

In my mind I was thinking, "Oh, it's finally over. I'll see the children." Anetta was praying and said, "Let's keep praying." We didn't want to eat. We didn't want to do anything. Twelve o'clock came, lunch time. Anetta was still praying. Just after 12:00 I was watching the TV by myself because all the rest of the people were in the cafeteria. I saw smoke right where my room was.[74] I remembered that before I left the men brought in some bales of hay and put them against the walls to provide insulation against the cold and to provide protection in case more shots were fired into the building. As the smoke continued getting thicker I was thinking, "What happened? They need to put some water on it." I had heard that sometimes bales of hay start burning by themselves. That was my first reaction; maybe this bale of hay had caught fire by itself. And I kept seeing the fire burning faster and spreading. I went running to the cafeteria to tell the people that Mount Carmel—the building was—on fire.

They came rushing out from the cafeteria to the room where the TV was. By that time other people were there. Anetta called me and the other believers. She said, "Let's go into the room and pray." We prayed on our knees in our room and went back.

From that point on it was a matter of watching the TV, standing there, watching . . . hoping for good news. As the fire was going on and on, I was asking myself, "Where is everyone? Is it over?" We watched the middle tower fall down, and we were standing there just hoping, just hoping that they had gotten out—that people were gone from that building. We couldn't see the back of the building. After the fire we were told that people were trying to go out the back and were being shot at.[75]

At that time on the television they were saying there were twenty survivors. In my heart I was going, "My children have come out"—the four children: Wayne, Anita, Sheila, and Lisa. I didn't worry about my husband because he had said he was going to stay until the end. He was going to make sure everyone else was out. He told me, "Don't be too alarmed if I choose to stay." He was trying to tell me not to be afraid, and just to know that everything was going to be okay. That's when he gave me a kiss on my cheek and said, "Goodbye," and went back into his office. I keep that memory. I keep the memory all the time of his walking away down the hallway.

When those of us who came out went downtown to the sheriff's office on the 21st of March, Daniel and Kimberly were there. Daniel, Kimberly, and I spoke with Wayne using a speaker phone. After that Wayne spoke with the negotiators. All he could talk about was the Bible, the Seven Seals, and getting to know God before it's too late. I recognized how important these truths were to Wayne. These are the things I have kept in my heart, that Wayne was so wanting the ATF and FBI agents to know God and to know the truth, and to know that they had but a short time, that God one day is going to change all this. These things have held me together even though his dying and suffering the most horrible death that I can think of is always with me. That was the last time I spoke with Wayne.

There's a movie showing people in a house that burned down. Two people were caught in the fire, and they show the bodies and the heads. Years ago I don't think I could have watched it. But I looked at it and said to myself, "I wonder if that's what they looked like. I hope not." But I realize it is so. There's another movie, *Waco: The Rules of Engagement*, that shows an actual person who was burned up at Mount Carmel. I don't want to see that. It's too close.

So I continued to watch the fire on the television at the Salvation Army halfway house. I remember the director was there. She was standing with us. She was holding on to Anetta. Anetta had a problem with her foot that made her knee buckle, so she was on crutches, standing there watching. Anetta and I left twice to pray. We were just hoping and hoping and hoping to the end.

After the fire was over we went into another room and sat down. On television they were talking again about twenty survivors. Then eventually they said there were only nine. Clive Doyle was one of those people. I wondered if Clive's daughter, Shari, got out,[76] if Anita was with her when everything started happening. We found out later that it was Rita Riddle's daughter, Misty Ferguson, and Marjorie Thomas and Ruth Riddle who survived.[77] The men who got out in addition to Clive were David Thibodeau, Jaime Castillo, Renos Avraam, Derek Lovelock, and Graeme Craddock.[78] David Thibodeau, Jaime, and Renos weren't hurt at all. Clive's hands and ankle were burned. Ruth Riddle and Marjorie were burned. Marjorie was burned the worst. Although my children did not survive, I was very happy for those who did make it out.

Marjorie Steps on Young Sheila

Clive came out of jail in February 1994 after he was acquitted in the criminal trial. In September 1994 we were on our way to Las Vegas. We were invited to be there at a gun convention. I never would have thought I'd be at such a strange thing. On that trip Clive said something about Marjorie, and then he said something about Sheila. I was going, "What? What? What are you saying?" He said Marjorie said that as she was coming out of the burning building she stepped on someone's fingers and that person went, "Ouch." Then Marjorie said, "Oh, I'm sorry." And the person said, "That's okay." Marjorie said that was my daughter Sheila. Apparently she was down on the floor. I started crying when I heard this. I was just totally overwhelmed by the fact that Sheila was alive. She was thinking of Marjorie. Marjorie cried and said, "I wish I had taken Sheila with me." She said, "I could have saved Sheila." But my first thought was that Marjorie was so badly burned. She has gone through so much pain. What if Sheila had escaped but was burned so badly that she was unhappy for the rest of her life, always thinking that she should have died? It just overwhelmed me. During the wrongful death trial in 2000 they mentioned Marjorie's statement about Sheila. I had to keep from crying in the courtroom or they would make me leave.

Through it all I could feel them. I could feel the flames. I could feel them standing against the walls. I could feel just everything that was happening to them. I felt that I knew the pain. Maybe their backs were to the fire and they were screaming. I could feel all the heat, and then I kept hoping that maybe the smoke got to them and that they died without knowing any pain. But then I thought of the people screaming. I can imagine so many things now, it's a horrible image that I face every day.

Immediately after the Fire

That first week after the fire I was in such pain over their deaths. I remember Gladys coming to sit with me at the Salvation Army halfway house on Sunday after church. I was on the top bunk and I felt like I was sinking down into the mattress. Gladys sat with me and I said, "Gladys, this is too much. This is horrible. I just can't get over how they died and they're gone." She kept encouraging me and I've never forgotten how she was there and sat and made me realize that God, who sees everything long beforehand, is here. It's like when you say, "I'm going to get on this boat because God says we're going to go right over there to that island," and then wind and rain come and we say, "That's not the kind of ride I thought we were going to have. It looked like a sunny, bright day but things started to get dark." That's what happened in my life. The weather changed.

We've read in the Bible that Job had the experience of losing his seven children, and God gave him back seven children. They weren't the same children who had died but God did give him more children. We believe God will bless in the long run. This is the kind of thing that I hold on to while I'm going through the experience of knowing that they died.

That week of the fire I felt like there was something pressing on my chest. Every day. There was a pain in the middle of my chest. I just didn't think I could go on, but Gladys helped me. And then my mother came and stayed a few days. She also went with me to the Salvation Army church. It was Mother's Day. They gave her a plant. I remember I was crying. My mother was crying, too. All those people reminded me of Mount Carmel. I just couldn't get over how I was in the same situation with a bunch of people, but they weren't the people I knew, the people I missed so very much. It was just a strange thing. All those people made me feel empty. It should have made me feel better to have so many people around. But I couldn't bear so many people while I was grieving so.

After a while I got better at being able to bear it. One of the ladies at the Salvation Army halfway house thought we should have been so distraught that we would be in the nuthouse. She said, "I can't believe you guys are able to deal with life this way. You should be just overwrought." I remember one man, who was one of the directors, said, "I want to talk to you because I need you to understand what's happened to you." I said, "Oh, I'm very aware. I know just what has happened here." He said, "I don't think so. You're not dealing with it the same way I think most people would. You should be screaming." I told him the Bible says we're not to grieve as others do. We're supposed to believe that God knows our needs and have the hope that we'll see our family again.

Meaning of the Events

In Mount Carmel we were reading and studying the scriptures concerning the future, and how God is going to let us be saved, this world is going to change, and we're going to, one day, live the way God wanted us to live in the beginning.

We knew some things were going to happen. We knew some things were not going to be good and we might be hungry or we might have to walk a long way, but we didn't expect to die. No one wanted to die, but we were willing. We knew that we'd be willing to accept whatever God said, but after awhile we thought, maybe we won't have to die, that God would have a different situation for us, and we would be there to be among the first people to help someone else.

I have kept in mind at least some of what we read in the Bible, what we studied with David, the things he said and how he treated us, and that has helped me so much now in living each day. David was always very patient. One time we had five bowls of half-eaten oatmeal in our room. David wanted us to keep our rooms clean, and take our things out to the kitchen. David must have walked around to check on something, and he looked in the room to see how everyone was, and I remember thinking, "Oh my God. Those bowls are in there." I thought he was going to say, "And what did I see up there in Sheila Martin's room? Bowls of cereal just sitting up there not being taken care of. Bad enough they weren't eaten but now they're just sitting there." I thought he was going to say that, but he didn't. And there were times when I thought he was not going to say anything, and he did say what he hated most about us. He'd say that he loved us, but didn't like what we did. He would tell us what God expected of us, but we didn't seem to change.

I think about how fair David was, and how I'm trying to live my life now. David always told us, never do anything out of anger. Always have a nice pleasant look on your face when you are around the children.[79] He didn't like to see frowns on our faces. He said, "I don't like to look around and notice that the parents are not saying anything, but they've got these horrible cross looks on their faces." He said, "I want you to show respect for the children always. Have an understanding of what God is like by the way you are with them, and by the look on your face."

AFTER THE FIRE

Seeing Jamie, Daniel, and Kimberly
for the First Time after the Fire

On Monday when the fire happened the first thing I wanted to do was call Child Protective Services. I told them that I wanted to see my children—Daniel and Kimberly and Jamie—the next day. They called me back and said they couldn't arrange it for Tuesday but they could for Wednesday. When we got there on Wednesday, the first thing said to me was, you are not to show any emotion. You are not to cry. These children are not to be made to feel bad in any way. If you do, we're going to take the children right back to the Methodist home. I had lost a husband and four children in the most horrible fire, but two days later I'm supposed to act like, "Oh, and guess what else happened? Let's put that aside. Let's do something else now and forget what happened."

Daniel was just six years old. He was the one who said to me, "Mommy, you know, my daddy and my brother and my sisters died in the fire." I wanted to reach out just so I could hold him. All I remember saying was, "Really, did they tell you that?" And he said, "Yes." And he went on to say something else about their deaths. I knew there was a mirror behind me where they were listening and watching to see what I was going to do, how I was reacting to him and whether I was going to make him cry.

Temporary Separation from Daniel and Kimberly

When I got to Child Protective Services on that Wednesday they brought me into a room where Wayne's parents were sitting at a table and there was another man there, maybe a psychologist, and the woman who brought me, and maybe one other person. I walked over and I hugged the grandparents. I said, "It's going to be okay. God said we'll see our loved ones again." This was my encouragement to them. The kids' grandfather asked me if I knew of any abuse going on at Mount Carmel. I said, "No." The kids' grandparents told me that Daniel and Kimberly were going back to New Jersey with them. On Thursday we were to have a memorial service at the Methodist Home chapel. We saw other Branch Davidian children who were sent out during the siege. On Friday the grandparents were going to take Daniel and Kimberly to Houston, and go from there to New Jersey. I asked, "Can you come by the Salvation Army place before you leave?" They came by and I had some candy for the kids and we said goodbye.

Sometime in May of '93 when I was at the Salvation Army halfway house, Mr. Coker, the attorney, and I went to the courthouse for a hearing. Child Protective Services was concerned about the kids coming back to live with me, and they discussed whether it was safe for them. I said I loved them. Finally the judge said, "Well, she doesn't have a job and she doesn't have a house for the kids." Did they tell me to have those things by that time? They decided to leave Daniel and Kimberly with the grandparents for a while longer.

Visiting Daniel and Kimberly in New Jersey

Afterwards I was told that in about three weeks or so I would get out of the halfway house. Toward the end of that period Child Protective Services called Wayne's parents and arranged for me to see Daniel and Kimberly on a Sunday from 2:00 p.m. to 5:00 p.m.

My sister picked me up in Connecticut after I had ridden to New York City and Connecticut on buses, and a few days later she and I drove to New Jersey so I could see the children. I had not been to the grandparents' new house before. After awhile I went in to fix Kimi's hair and wash her face. When we came back out, Daniel was kind of rough and tumble. I tried to get him settled down. After sitting outside for a while, we went to McDonald's to get some food.

The grandparents took Daniel and Kimi back home after we ate at McDonald's. My sister and her little boy and I were in my sister's car. Kimi was sitting on her grandmother's lap crying. I heard her grandmother say, "She has to go back so she can get a house for you to live in."

The Salvation Army people had told me that after I visited the children that I was to go up to Boston to stay with my mother. Once I got to Boston I was supposed to go to a parole office; I was supposed to check in with them because during the time I was a material witness I was supposed to let them know where I was.

My mother and I went down to the parole office together. The woman there said to us that if we were found to have a gun, even if someone threw that gun in our yard, that we would both have to go to jail. They were going to take my mother, too! My mother and I started crying. My mother said, "I don't understand. This doesn't make sense." So I said, "I want to go back to Texas." The officer said I could go back to Waco for testing to get the children back eventually.

I was in Boston on Wednesday. By Friday I was on a plane flying back to Texas. I couldn't bear to be in Boston. God reminded me, "Jamie is there in Texas. You should be there with him. It would be good to see him. Why should he be there by himself?"

Returning to Waco to Make a Home

When I came back to Waco I went to stay at the Brittany Hotel. After the fire, the man who owned the Brittany Hotel, Mark Domangue, went over to the Salvation Army and told them he was willing to give our people a place to stay. He said he was willing to offer a place for us to stay until we found other places to live. He said he had plenty of rooms at the hotel. Catherine Matteson, Rita Riddle, and Janet McBean[80] were there as well as some others.

The next day or so, the guy from the parole office came in and said to me, "What are you doing here in Texas?" I said, "They told me I could come back." He said, "Okay. I guess you can stay here in Waco." I had to come once a week to the parole office as if I were a criminal just released from jail.

Television Talk Shows

Mark Domangue made arrangements with the people from the Maury Povich show to tape a show with us in early November in Waco.[81] I remember a lady coming up at the end of the taping who said to me, I can't believe you left your children inside. I told her about how we were all supposed to go out. The children were going to the Methodist Children's Home when they came out. They wanted to be at Mount Carmel. They believed in it. By the time I finished telling her, she said she felt a little differently. She said, "I realize you didn't just leave your children. You loved them after all."

Geraldo Rivera wanted me to be on his show. They were going to work it out so I could go see Daniel and Kimberly. They said they were going to arrange it. I don't know if that really was going to happen. They kept telling me that as an incentive to come. Rita Riddle said, "All those people are going to be mean. They're going to be putting you down." I didn't go.

But I always spoke to reporters whenever I was asked. As many times as I could speak, I did. Every once in a while, after two or three years went by, I started to say no, only because I wanted my story to be told truthfully.

Learning to be the Head of the Family

I found a house to rent two weeks after coming back to Waco. I found the house I rented by looking in one of those Thrifty Nickel–type of papers. Kathy Jones had driven me by there to see the house.

Wayne had taken care of me, and David took care of us after that, so I didn't have a clue about many things. Mark Domangue's wife took me over to the bank. I kept saying, "I've got to hold on to a little money." Social Security had given us $250 for Wayne's death. That was just the amount I needed for the security deposit. At the real estate office I took two steps towards the desk to give my money and sign the lease when a man came in the door asking to rent the same house. If I had been any slower I would not have gotten the house!

After I rented the house people started giving me things to furnish it with. Bonnie gave me some beds. I got sheets and spreads. A lady from Denton, Texas, came down and took me places and bought food for me and gave many other things. Another woman came down from Weatherford, Texas, and helped drive me around. Many people from the Dallas area helped us. I was ready to get the children.

But Child Protective Services was still not telling me I could have the kids back. Finally in September they sent me a letter saying they were going to have a meeting concerning the children. They decided they were going to let Jamie come stay with me first, but they would not let Daniel and Kimberly come yet. They said they wanted me to get used to having Jamie. Jamie came on the 28th of September.

In 1984 when I visited Mount Carmel for the first time, I traveled with Jamie by myself. Jamie was not quite two years old, and Wayne stayed in North Carolina with the four older children. Then all those years later, in 1993, Wayne and the four children were gone—they had died. The other two children were up in New Jersey with Wayne's parents. And I was here in Texas by myself with Jamie. It was so strange that this situation kept repeating: Wayne and the kids were someplace else. They had died together and they were gone.

Toward the end of October, Kimi and Daniel came. I went up and met them at the airport in Dallas. Daniel and Kimberly had stayed with their grandparents six and a half months. It seemed like forever.

We lived in the house that I rented for three and a half years, and during that time Jamie road the bus to school. I learned how to take Daniel and Kimberly back and forth to school in the car. I had to learn how to drive in Waco—it was a bigger city than Palestine. I didn't drive the whole five years we were at Mount Carmel. I never needed to drive when I was there. I could ride with people and show them the way, but I never drove. I always rode with Wayne or Perry. Now that I was on my own I was scared to death to drive. One time I couldn't even back out of the driveway because I was scared. I thought people would look at me making mistakes. Since then I have driven to both the East and West coasts.

The Criminal Trial

We waited for the criminal trial to start. We went to San Antonio in February 1994. I did not get to go into the court-room until the last day of the trial. Then they called us back a couple of days later for the verdict. Clive Doyle was acquitted of all charges and returned to Waco with his mother, Edna Doyle.[82]

Resumed Branch Davidian Gatherings

Clive and Edna were back in Waco with the families and friends of all of us who had taken up the cause. Sometime in late May or June 1994, Clive asked, "Do you think we could have some studies at your house?" That is when we started having Bible studies at my house. People started coming and we had ten, fifteen people sometimes for our studies on Saturday afternoons.

The Burials

The place where they chose to put the bodies of our family members was a paupers' field in Waco that never had any tombstone markers. When you went there you saw a place where maybe one marker was way over across the field, so you'd think there were just a few people buried there. We were never told that they were getting ready to bury some of our people. After they buried Novellette Sinclair we saw it mentioned in the news, and they made it sound like no one was there for the burial because no one cared. We didn't even know it was happening.

The authorities had kept the bodies in a freezer in Fort Worth. The government needed autopsies done, which they said would prove our people did things—shot people, killed each other, or shot or stabbed little children. So the bodies stayed up in Fort Worth. We saw body bags on the news. They wanted to say there weren't that many people. Then they said, oh, we think there were as many people as David said. Some of them were burned together, holding each other. That's when they began to realize that they had to count more people. Sometimes they were putting two or three in one bag. They began to realize, yes, there are as many as seventy-four people dead.

At some point the freezer was turned off.[83] Then things started to melt and the bodies became nothing. They decided they didn't need them up there and sent them down here to Waco.

I got a phone call on a Saturday morning telling me they were burying our loved ones out at the cemetery. I rushed to pick up some of our people and get out there. When we got there we saw yellow tape around some trees, and we were told not to go past the tape.

Clive and Edna Doyle were able to get over there quickly. I picked up Catherine Matteson and Margaret Lawson. Other people who knew us came out. There were other people there who weren't part of our group but who lived close by. I think that's one of the reasons God brought them to live close by, because when the time came they found out about the burials.

We came and saw the "Do Not Cross" yellow tape around the trees. We also saw a lot of cars coming in, men putting coffins in the ground very quickly, and the cars zooming off again. I'm wondering, "Where's the funeral where you sit down and the minister is there and you're underneath a tent to keep you dry?" It was kind of a rainy day and we were wondering why we weren't having that kind of funeral. We had gone to the health department and different places to apply for these burials, and we had to sign our names saying we didn't have the money to bury them, but still I didn't think it was going to be that horrible kind of burial.

All I remember is how fast it was and that there were no small coffins. They were all adult-sized coffins. The children were in the same-sized coffins as the adults.[84] The only time we saw a small coffin at that place was when Jamie died five years later. Jamie is buried in the same row with his father, brother, and sisters. They said there was space there when he died in February 1998.

We were standing there, watching all this, and newspaper reporters asked us how we felt. We said we felt horrible. This was in September 1994, a year and a half since they had died.

We just hated the fact that there was no respect for our loved ones. The people operating the backhoes were there. They said it used to be a place that was a dump. Clive said there were old mattresses thrown out there. I know that just because our people were put into a paupers' cemetery they weren't paupers, and they will rise as kings and queens.

At first, I think all they left as markers were little metal things with numbers. Eventually they started putting little marble markers there. They don't all have names on them. One of them says, "Unknown Martin."[85] Some of the autopsies showed that they just found pieces of different people. They didn't know to whom the body parts belonged; they just found them in a hallway or some place where the person had died. Some they could identify right away. The young children and their mothers were found in the vault at Mount Carmel.[86] I wondered where my children were found.

Trip Out West

In 1996 I took Kimi and Daniel to California. We were going to meet Clive and a few others at Lake Tahoe where he was giving a speech at a convention. I left Jamie at a respite center in Copperas Cove, Texas. We kept in touch by phone. Previously I had to return to get Jamie when I was in Washington, D.C. in 1995 for the congressional hearings. I was hoping this time would be different.

We drove to the Grand Canyon and then to Las Vegas. There was a family there who supported the Branch Davidians, and we were invited to stay with them, and also with another family who were supporters. My brother also lived in Las Vegas and we saw him briefly. After a few days we were on our way to San Diego to visit the zoo.

On the way there we had some car trouble. Janet McBean, who lived in California, came to pick us up and took us to her place. While I was at her place the respite center called me: "Come and check on your boy." They wanted to put a feeding tube in him and I didn't want it. Kimi and Daniel stayed with Janet while I flew back to Texas and checked on

Jamie. I took him to his doctor at Scott and White Hospital in Temple, Texas. They observed him for a day, and then they said I could take him home. After I got home I tried to decide what I was going to do next. I decided to rent a car and drive back to California with Jamie. I drove past El Paso into New Mexico. We stayed overnight and then drove to Phoenix, Arizona. I had to get another rental car there to continue on to California. It was very hot and I had to carry all the bags plus Jamie in my arms to the next rental area. Believe me, I was very happy to get back on the road again.

I didn't intend on this trip to have to return to Texas on a plane and drive back again to California. But this is where we were and I believed God would take care of us on the road. I was able to feed Jamie and take care of all his needs. No matter what situation you are in, God is there for you. If you are determined you will succeed. I'm just thankful I did it. I have less opportunity to travel now, but at the time I was wanting to forget so much of what had happened just a couple of years earlier.

Jamie and I got to California where Daniel and Kimi were with Janet. The next day we went over to my niece's house and she had passes for us to go to Universal Studios.

Experiencing the Fire: Backdraft

My niece took care of Jamie the first day and I took Kimi and Daniel to Universal Studios. We went into the *Backdraft* exhibition. They had recreated the set of the movie, *Backdraft*, which is about firefighters.[87] At some point you are led into a room and you stand and wait for the next step of the exhibit. It immediately got hot. I tried to figure out what was wrong. Was the air conditioner not working? The doors opened and then I understood what was next. It was a recreation of what was in the finale of the movie. On a big stage men were fighting and the fire was coming up. It started getting hotter and you saw flames, and all of a sudden I felt I was in that building at Mount Carmel. I thought, "This is what it was like for them." Remember now, every time I saw the Mount Carmel fire on TV, all I saw was a building burning with no noise. In this *Backdraft* place where I was standing, I was hearing the crackling of the fire. I heard things falling down. It was just too much. It was more real than all the years I had watched the Mount Carmel fire on TV or in movies, because I was feeling flames. I was hearing noises. Fortunately, I did not hear people screaming. Then we went out. I don't think Daniel and Kimi were as affected by it as I was.

The next day we came back to Universal Studios because we had a pass for another day. On that day I brought Jamie in his wheelchair and we moved it around as best we could. That was the last time we all went on a trip together. Two years later Jamie was gone.

Jamie's Death

When I went on trips I left Jamie in a respite center, but they couldn't feed him very well. So by 1996 I decided it was time for us to stay close to Waco. We stayed home and didn't get to go on as many trips. Jamie always had more trouble with his health in the winter, and each winter that passed his health deteriorated more.

My dear, lovey boy went to his rest on February 11, 1998. He was remembered with a little garden called Jamie's Place at his school that he attended for five years. The teachers of the school attended his funeral. I am sorry he never recovered completely from his handicaps, but I know that when he is healed in the kingdom we will rejoice.

For years until Jamie's death I had always needed to know how to travel with or without him. Now the burden of how to do it was gone, but it was still always in the back of my mind as to what was the best for Jamie in each situation. Even on the day of his funeral, when we were about to eat I thought of what was there to feed him with easily.

Many times we were visiting places and Jamie wasn't with us, but he was never far from my thoughts. Now we were going to resume our visits without having a deadline to get back for him.

Resuming Family Life and Activities

We continued to visit the Branch Davidians in various prisons and different relatives for a while. But I needed to secure a better way of providing for Daniel and Kimberly. I had purchased a home. There were many mounting bills. I still wanted to stay home with Kimi and Daniel, but saw the time slipping away. They and I were getting older.

WORK

With the money from Wayne's Social Security death benefit slowly being withdrawn as the children came to ages sixteen and eighteen, it became very necessary for me to begin finding a way to provide for the children when this money would be stopped. While we were receiving money each month it felt as if Wayne was still providing for us, just as he had always done. Of course, I was very aware he was not merely away sending money home to us, but he didn't seem so distant as long as we were being provided for.

Just at the point when I needed to start working, Ofelia Santoyo told me of an opportunity to assist a woman living in the Salvation Army retirement center and be paid by a health care service. I also started caring for another woman at the retirement center. I enjoyed working with the elderly at the Salvation Army retirement center. After I worked there for two years I was able to apply for a job at the daycare center I passed every day as I took Kimberly to the Adventist school. As I would drive past it I realized I wouldn't have to make double trips to the church school and my job if I worked there.

The first woman I assisted at the retirement center was very sympathetic to our experience and always spoke well of the children. The people at the retirement center treated me very well. I was so encouraged. I found it hard to leave but because I now had a Certified Nursing Assistant certificate I wanted to work with children. The CNA certificate has helped me with taking care of the children. Their medications, temperatures, and daily care are so much a necessary part of each day at work. I feel very thankful I live close to the community college and was able to work a few hours in the day and go to school in the evening to obtain my certificate.

The Daycare Center

I'm very proud to say that I am a teacher at a Christian daycare center. I get to be with all the age groups, including the babies, which I enjoy very much. We have infants from six weeks up to children five years old, each age group in a separate room. The teachers are all different nationalities and cultures and backgrounds. Because it is in a Christian setting we believe that God has helped us to grow together and learn to do things together.

The children I care for have been a great help and comfort to me, and I pray for them and their families, because I come from a place where there was so much death and so many children having to die so horribly. What I see daily is little children so alive—living and bouncing around and full of life. It comforts and encourages me, and I pray that these same little children will one day be in the kingdom. Through my job I have gotten to know people that I would never have known.

It bothered me at first that each year a group of children left my room to go into another room. I felt like I was losing children again that I had come to love, but now I understand it as part of their growing and my growing, too.

We're getting more children who aren't completely well. They have seizures and they have medicines. We're becoming more like nurses than just people who change diapers. I'm hoping, if it is God's will, that there will be more money given to the people who are doing the best they can to take care of their families.

I feel like God has been very gracious to give me a chance to know all these people and see their lives, some who are struggling and some who are doing very well. It's a mixture of people all working together. God bless them all.

Being the Breadwinner and Homeowner

I try to take care of my children, and get them through school, have a car, house, clothes and food, all the things my husband took care of and did for us when he was alive. I keep thinking that if there could be just a little bit more money we would not have to be afraid or worry. I still wish it were my husband being the breadwinner, and I could have stayed home with the children.

On October 16, 2002, I was called to work for the daycare center. It has been quite an experience in many ways. I want people to be glad I have been there. That I have shown a Christian spirit in all that I do is very important to me and, I'm sure, to God. I have been a person who will be there when they don't have anyone else. Even when I take a day off, they know I'll be there if they need me.

I still believe it's all up to God, who will allow me to have whatever I need for this life and our life to come.

I can't forget the neighbors I have known these past fourteen years. Some have moved. Many have died for different reasons. I believe God saw ahead and knew where I should be while we have been waiting for the next step in our journey home.

REMEMBERING THE LOVED ONES
WHO DIED IN 1993

I remember my family, and I often wonder what people would think of my husband and children if they had the chance to live again.

Wayne had a wonderful laugh and a beautiful smile. He had a great sense of humor. I keep thinking of different types of foods he liked, and how before he came to Mount Carmel he would say no to this, maybe a small piece of that. After we got to the Palestine camp and Mount Carmel we were eating greens and vegetables and salads and things that he probably would never have wanted, but something about being out in that fresh air, I guess, perked up his appetite.

Wayne wanted to serve God and find out why I wanted to be a part of the Branch Davidians for so long. I think Wayne realized this had to be something special and he wanted to be a part of it. I'm very thankful that God brought him into my life.

Sometimes I don't want to remember things because I find it hard to think of how much we had at that time and I miss it so much, but at some point my heart says, "I want to remember, to think of the good things."

I think of Wayne and the time we went over to his office in Waco and he had a watermelon sitting on his desk—this big fancy lawyer with the office and a watermelon sitting on his desk for his lunch. Once in a while when I have to go in that building, I'll go up on the second floor and look around the corner to where his door was, and I think how I would love to go back to those years, to be back with him sitting in that office with his car out in that parking lot.

Anita, being 18, was the big sister so she was always trying to tell Lisa, the thirteen year old, how to do things. I remember Anita wanting to take care of Daniel as a baby. She always wanted to give him a bath and do things for him. I often wonder what it would be like now for Anita to be in her thirties as the older sister. I remember a tall, beautiful young woman who liked nice clothes and enjoyed reading her Bible. Michele Jones and Shari Doyle were her friends.

Anita and I went to the Department of Public Safety once to get her an I.D. for school and renew my driver's license. We decided to go into the bathroom to fix our hair before we had the pictures taken. Anita was so much taller than me so she chose to help me. As she was brushing my hair she commented, "People won't know who's the mother and who's the daughter." Remembering these little things from time to time makes me laugh, even though it also makes me sad.

Little Wayne was always trying to learn new things. He was learning to drive the trucks at Mount Carmel, as well as painting and construction. He was very much into the Bible truths. He understood many things about the Bible. He studied every day. At age five he could read out loud in the Bible studies. At age seven he knew how to repeat the names of all the books of the Bible and when he visited Sunday churches he always won prizes for knowing so many things. He would read the Sabbath school lessons and look up scriptures in the Bible, and this helped him immensely. David was very impressed with little Wayne's understanding and he believed the Holy Spirit was with him.

Little Wayne was the most respectful boy and young man. When he became a teenager, he would point out the right things for me to do. Little Wayne wanted to serve God and it was something he was very faithful in doing. David was very proud of him.

Little Wayne attended McLennan Community College in Waco, majoring in history. His father was very impressed with his intelligence and love for God.

Lisa is the hardest one for me to think of how she died. She was a sweet, loving girl, always helping me with the youngest children. She stayed in the room with Jamie, Kimberly, Daniel, and myself. Her bed was in the corner of the room and I would look over at different times of the night and see her sleeping. On other nights I could hear her laughter down the hallway. She was the last child I saw in the chapel listening to Steve Schneider giving a study about going to jail. I expected her to be at the Methodist Children's Home. I still think of that when we pass by there sometimes. She was so very cute.

Lisa took care of Bobbie Lane, the youngest child of David and Rachel. Bobbie Lane was just a young baby, but she was able to call Lisa's name. I still can see Lisa walking down the hallway with Bobbie on her hip.

Lisa has a cousin who was born four months before she was. When the cousin reaches different ages and experiences I think maybe Lisa would be sharing in doing the same things. Jamie also has a cousin born three months after he was. When I hear their mothers speak of their children I hurt, but I am glad they still have their children.

Anita and Wayne were close in age and then Sheila and Lisa were close in age.

I remember Sheila wanting to do a lot of cooking and babysitting. When she turned thirteen or fourteen I didn't see her as much. She went to live on the other side of the building, upstairs with a few other people. Before that I fixed her hair, and she played with the other children. She had a beautiful smile.

At Mount Carmel I would walk with Larry Sylvia for exercise and at first Sheila walked with us. We walked slowly. The Bible says the first shall be last, and the last shall be first. We would sing that song just so we wouldn't feel so badly as the others ran past us. After the second day, Sheila said, "You know, you aren't going to lose any weight this way. You guys walk too slow." The next day she left us. She said she had to walk faster. I remember running one time with Sheila and another person on the other side who said, "Sheila, your mom is keeping up with us." She smiled.

Lisa, at 13, was the only one who didn't have any problem with her weight. The rest of us were out there walking and running. Lisa would get up and help me with the younger children and then she would go over to Michele Jones' room and help with her children. After the ATF raid, when all the shooting was finished, I asked Lisa where she had been. She was in the room with Michele with the shots coming into the room through the walls. She said they were on the floor, as low as they could be, and in the corners. There was no place to hide; there were only four walls and beds in that room.

I often think about what it would be like with all these personalities in the same room, at this age, with Daniel being 21 and Kimi being 18. Kimi will still cry once in a while when she thinks of their birthdays. She will say, "I never knew them. I wish I could know them now." She says, "I was so young. The time I had with them, those four years weren't the same if I could have them now, from 14 to 18." I try to remember good things to tell Kimi about our times together.

Our kids liked being at Mount Carmel. They liked staying up until 3:00, 4:00, 5:00, and 6:00 a.m. watching movies and reading the Bible and getting pizza and sodas and ice cream. It was a life they were all very pleased with. I was happy to know they were down the hallway laughing. They were learning as much as other kids. They went to the laundry and watched MTV to keep up with new music videos. They were normal teenagers. It was a life that I was very happy that they had. They met people from different countries and cultures, and learned how to eat different foods, and how to live with different kinds of people.

One of the comforts that I have in these last few years is that I remember how David said that our lives are going to go from glory to glory. There is never going to be a place where we will stop learning or gaining. Seeing our family members again, holding them, and rejoicing that they are alive will be just the first step. Then we're going to be building up the kingdom. Eventually, they are supposed to have families and they will go off to other worlds. This is the glory to glory. If David hadn't encouraged us to think of these things I would always be distraught over what has happened, the fact that they are dead, there are no grandchildren, there are no homes to visit, as I see other people have in their lives.

David told us that we are all going to be able to be in the kingdom. I want to see them gain that. I want to see them rejoice. I want to see their mates and their families. And that's so much more than the small amount of time that we aren't with them. Eternity is forever. We'll always have that joy. The joy of their faces and the joy of seeing everyone in one place in one heart, one belief, are going to be with us forever.

After the fire there were many things the survivors were left without. I lost these loved ones and I hate to think of the horror of the way they died. But I am also given a lot of hope. I'll always remember those beautiful smiles. I am thankful for the beautiful pictures of the children. I am looking forward to what God's going to do in the future.

REFLECTIONS ON THE LOSS OF LOVED ONES

I was told that a lot of firefighters here in Waco weren't allowed to go to Mount Carmel in 1993; they weren't allowed to put out the fire. But on 9/11 the media reported on the men who died, how they willingly went into the buildings. The firefighters in Waco would have done the same thing. They would have tried to save our family. The firefighters were so close to us, yet none of them were able to help when we needed them. I kept asking, "Why?" It was years before I told my mother. I said, "Mother, they kept them back."[88] They were not allowed to help. She couldn't believe it. All this time she was thinking that no one was there to help, that there was no way to put out the fire.

When we were in Palestine, Texas, we used to have time every morning for worship when we'd sit and read the psalms. One of the psalms says, we spend our years as a tale that is told (Psalm 90:9), and David said that one of these days we're going to live all these psalms. We were reading psalms in the Bible when we were at the Salvation Army halfway house and we were reminded of that.

People have said that God hides things from us because we'd shrink at what would happen and would not go forward if we knew. But when I see how God has brought us through, I'm able to go through other things in faith, and hopefully help other people. It means a lot when people stop me and say, "I know who you are. If it wasn't for you, I couldn't get through this problem I have. I thought of you when your husband died. Now my husband has died and I'm able to be strong." It's worth knowing that other people are helped by my tragedy.

In 1995, when the Oklahoma City bombing happened, they asked me, "Are there words you can give to the mothers whose children were lost in the explosion?" I said, "The only thing I can say is that God will be with you. I know that it will still hurt many years from now. It's been two years since the fire and it still hurts. It's going to hurt for a long time."

Before I did not understand why people still cried for their deceased children thirty, forty years later. I couldn't understand then, but I do now. That hurt just still stays and wells up in you.

KEEPING THE FAITH

David Koresh as Christ

David said that whenever you're in a situation where someone comes to you and helps you and brings you up from where you are to a better state of mind, where someone makes you think better and want to live a better life, you can consider that person a messiah. David said that Jamie was a messiah to my husband and myself. Jamie gave us an incentive to live better, to want to do better.

So I can't see why saying a person is a messiah has to be something bad. Anybody can be a messiah for someone. David has been and continues to be that for me, because every day, even at my job, I think of the things he encouraged us to be, and I try my best to let people see that, so by knowing me they know a little bit more about what David was like. If I am kind and generous and considerate, then my time with the people at Mount Carmel has not taken that away from me, but has added to whoever I was before I went there.

I just wish other people didn't have to struggle with losses and problems the way I have had to struggle. But I think God sometimes wants us to see what other people are going through. David said that all of us who were with him, whatever station of life we're in, at the time of judgment are going to be able to talk with and judge another person who has been in the same situation, and they can be saved because we've been through it and can say, "I know why they did this," or "I know what they went through." We will be the judges to help the other people get through, and they can be comforted, knowing that we know and understand.

Some people say that Christ doesn't live in this time, he lived way back then. David said that's why he was here as the Christ, because he knows what it is like to live here, eat ice cream and things that taste so good, and want things so much. He said someone had to be here at this time, so people could understand and say, "I relate to you."

Reunion in God's Kingdom

I'll do just as Job did—one day I'll reap the joy of my children. They'll be in my arms. But I also know that very soon after that they will be starting their lives and they'll be going to planets and universes. Just when I get kind of settled in the new life that we'll have in the kingdom, we're going to be moving about again.

I just thank God that I'm able to look back on the pain and the suffering and the horror, and the feeling that I've done something differently from most other people, and be sustained by the hope that if I continue believing that God is my father, my husband, my maker, that I will also reap the joys of what he has for us in the future, and then he will make it all worth it. Christ had to believe that. That's why he came and died. So we have to believe that our family members have lived and died so we can believe even better.

The disciples knew the faith they had, they knew the courage they had in knowing Christ when he was on Earth 2,000 years ago. We have that same comfort in David, knowing what we've learned and what we've been able to experience with him.

When I came out of Mount Carmel in 1993 there was money left in my husband's bank account, which helped me get a car, and then later other people helped me when I was trying to buy a house. A lot of people helped us in so many ways. People continue to strengthen us by the way they are interested, and the way they try to comfort us. They have gone through painful experiences and they know it still hurts them, so they know we are still hurting. But our comfort is in knowing that we are going to see our family members because God has promised these things, and we continue on with that hope.

The main thing I remember through it all is that God has been our strength and has helped us in so many ways, in all the ways that we can possibly be helped, and I know God is not finished with us yet. He still has better things for us.

I just want to say that I'm very, very thankful. I don't think I've gained enough insight yet from these experiences. It has been especially precious for people to say that what happened at Mount Carmel was not right: It should not have happened, let me see what I can do. To think that when I call and talk with my mother, I can say, yes, all these things happened as the result of our being a part of this church, yes, it has been a lot of horror, but there have been a lot of good things. I think she has been very impressed with that. As I look over all the things that have happened in my life, I see how God has been very gracious. I have met so many people in so many different walks of life, and I'm just thankful for the day God said I had more to learn and thought of me long before I knew him. My life was turned around for eternity.

Our children are a gift from God. They are only lent to us for a little while. I remember when they were mine.

Drawing 1: Sheila uses the words of a popular song to express her feelings of loss for her five oldest children, young Wayne, Anita, young Sheila, and Lisa, who died in the fire in 1993, and the smallest one, Jamie, whose growth was stunted by the meningitis he contracted when he was four months old and who died in 1998. They are depicted going through a door with their backs to Sheila. The picture of the unicorn sketched on the left represents David Koresh, the Christ.

Drawing 2: This drawing depicts the buses and cottages at the Palestine camp in which people lived as well as the building in which they cooked and ate. The bus in the center clearing is the Martin bus.

Drawing 3: This drawing shows Sheila, Daniel and Kimberly hiding behind a bed in their room when the shootout with the ATF agents began. Daniel asks, "Why did the bad men come?" Jamie is lying on the couch in front of the window where the gunshots are coming in. The caption next to Jamie reads, "Jamie is blind, screaming at the top of his lungs." Sheila wonders, "How do I reach Jamie? Is this the way I lose him?" The bed in the right corner is labeled "Lisa's bed." Lisa, 13, had recently moved upstairs.

Drawing 4: Depiction of Sheila holding Jamie, hiding with Daniel and Kimberly behind the bed during the shootout with the ATF agents. Daniel asks, "Why did the bad men come?

Drawing 5: The death of a Branch Davidian mother, Jaydean Wendel, during the shootout with the ATF agents is depicted. Bullets can be seen coming through the window. Jaydean is shot while she is lying in the top bunk. The caption reads: "On February 28, 1993, Jaydean Wendell was killed. She had four children. One child was only four months old. During the attack they sat on the floor outside their bedroom; another woman was there to comfort them." One of the children asks, "Where's Mommy?" The oldest child, Jaunessa, says, "Mommy's not here."

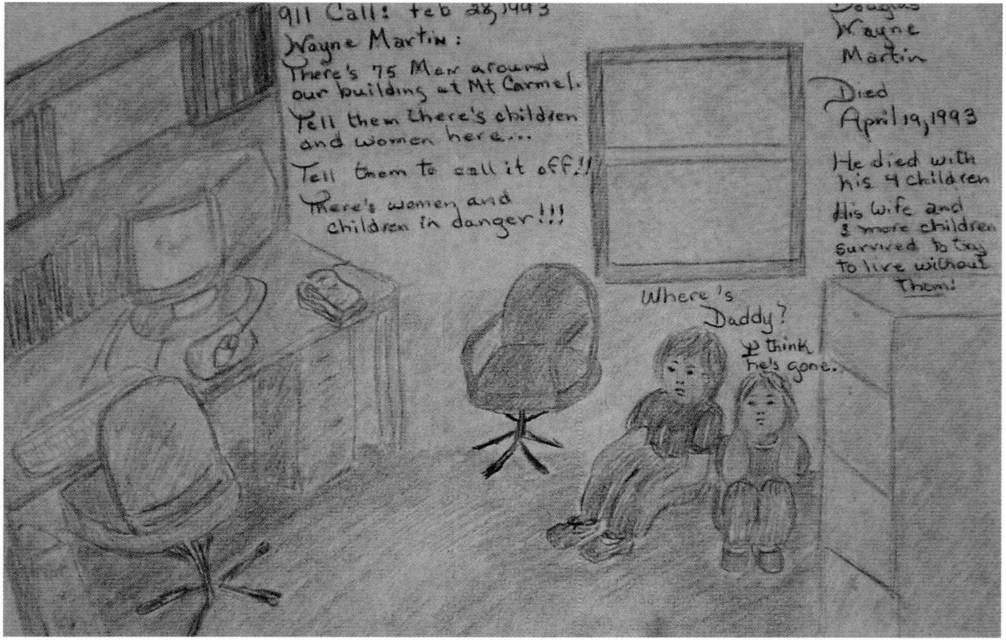

Drawing 6: Daniel and Kimberly sit in their father's office.

Drawing 7: The deceased Wayne Martin depicted with all of his deceased children, young Wayne, Anita, young Sheila, Jamie on his lap, and Lisa.

Drawing 8: David Koresh is depicted with all the children who died in the fire, his biological children, as well as the others. The caption reads, "He loved them all," and the children's names are given.

Drawing 9: This drawing shows the wounded David Koresh lying on the floor in the hallway on an upper floor at Mount Carmel surrounded by women and children. This scene depicts March 2 when the Branch Davidians were supposed to come out but then David informed the FBI agents that God had told him that they should wait.

Drawing 10: The deceased children looking at a newspaper dated April 19, 1993, with the headline, "Tragedy in Waco," ask, "Does it say we all died?" The concrete vault in which they died is sketched in outline in the background.

Drawing 11: In this drawing the children who died at Mount Carmel in the fire are simultaneously inside the residence (with David Koresh's guitars and chair in the background) and looking over the residence from the outside, saying, "This was our home!"

Drawing 12: The deceased children of Mount Carmel are depicted here with the burning building in the lower lefthand corner saying, "We didn't want to die," and "We did . . . April 19, 1993."

Drawing 13: The words of a popular song are used to ask, "Where have all the children gone?" The children's play area on the left is contrasted with the tank and the burning building on the right.

Drawing 14: A depiction of life at Mount Carmel "Before 'They' Came."

Drawing 15: Idyllic "Some Times We Remember," of children and their mothers playing in the pool.

Drawing 16: The deceased children of Mount Carmel say, "We just wanted to play . . . But. . . ."

Drawing 17: The deceased children locate each one's crape myrtle tree and memorial stone. "This is our row." "Mine is over here." "I think this one is mine." "Mommy's is here."

Drawing 18: The deceased Branch Davidian children are examining the large memorial stone listing the names of all the Branch Davidians who died in 1993. They are standing in the grove of crape myrtle trees planted for each deceased Branch Davidian.

Drawing 19: The deceased children with their respective deceased mothers are depicted above the concrete vault labeled, "This Is Where We All Died, April 19th."

Drawing 20: This picture depicts the multiracial group of people from England who died at Mount Carmel. The caption reads, "America Did This!" The memorial stone below indicates that Winston Blake died on February 28, 1993, and that on April 19, 1993, "All the rest burned."

Drawing 21: This drawing entitled "You Burn It!! We Build It!!" depicts in the upper left the only remaining structures after the fire on April 19, 1993: the cylindrical metal water tower and the concrete vault in which the young children and their mothers died. The structure drawn in pencil on the right, labeled "Mt. Carmel, April 19, 2000," is the chapel constructed on the site by volunteers.

Drawing 22: This drawing depicts clusters of surviving Branch Davidian children who lost parents in the 1993 conflict. Their deceased parents are listed by name. These portraits surround a depiction of the large memorial stone at Mount Carmel that gives the names of all the Branch Davidians who died in 1993.

Drawing 23: This drawing contains several portraits of David Koresh along with the unicorn, which symbolizes David as the only male in the community who was supposed to procreate children.

Drawing 24: Portrait of David Koresh with his guitar.

Drawing 25: "Our 23 Children, 1–18 yrs. April 19th 1993. We're Gone . . . But Not for Long," expresses the belief that the children are part of the "wave sheaf," consisting of people totally committed to God who will be resurrected with David and return with him during the Endtime events to create God's kingdom.

Appendix

SHEILA MARTIN'S DRAWINGS

Sometimes as time goes on you begin to forget things. You begin to not feel the intensity of your emotions at that time, how much of a burden it was for you to go through all those things. You have a tendency to remember just the biggest things when there are a lot of little things that people want to hear about, also. They want to understand what was happening through the time of the ATF raid, the siege, after I came out and went to jail, then the Salvation Army halfway house, and then trying to make a home. I thought that the best thing to do was to put it all down on paper in drawings. Sometimes I just knew what I wanted to draw. I woke up in the middle of the night and said, "I want to draw that, and I don't want to forget this." After a while I had so many drawings, I began to say, "Is this enough? Have I shown enough things?" I made these drawings between 1998 and 2000. Most of the drawings were done in 2000.

In the drawings of the children, they are not alive but I have drawn them as appearing alive. They are asking questions about themselves, such as in drawing 10 where the children are standing around a newspaper asking, "Does it say we all died?" Maybe some of these ideas came from the movies, such as showing people looking at themselves at a funeral. I ended up realizing what a horror it would be to be dead and to know that so many things happened and you are still seeing, you are still witnessing. My intention is to cause the viewer to be shocked enough to say, "They were just little children."

When I go back and look at the drawings a lot of feelings come back. Some of it I could only imagine at a time when things were still so fresh in my mind. I am just so thankful that I did look into these things and draw. Once you get busy with the cares of this world and trying to stay alive and keep things going, all of these things that were so precious to you get lost. They would have become lost if I hadn't made the drawings.

Drawing 1 came to me in the middle of the night when I decided to draw a picture of my children who died. They are leaving. They are going out the door. It is as if they just walked out. They had a little brother who died many years later, but I chose to put him there also. The song goes, "Where are you going, my little ones, my little ones? Where are you going, my little babes of mine?"

I remember coming out of Mount Carmel in 1993, and turning and looking back at the building. That was my one last look. In this picture I turned around, and they weren't my babes any more. That's what it was. I walked out the door and walked up the road to a man who was in the tank. That's always going to be my memory. That was the last time I saw them. The building in one piece, I walked out the front door, knowing that all the people were in the chapel talking. I went out the door. I drew a picture of my children going out the door, but it's the same thing as their walking away from me. Their backs are toward me. I can't see their faces.

The day before yesterday I thought, "I can't feel them anymore." Right after the fire, I could feel their bodies being burned. I could feel the heat on their backs. I felt every bit of heat on my back, because I could only imagine they were bending over, trying to protect themselves. That's why their backs are toward me in the picture. I can't see their faces, and I can't see their faces now.

Drawing 2 depicts the camp at Palestine, Texas. When we first arrived, there were only buses in which people were living. Every time David came back from a trip to California or some other place he would build something. One time he built a building where we ate and worshiped and he would play music. We had a lot of Sister White's books there, and there was some furniture so we could go in and sit. Later a little kitchen was built on the side. Each time David came there was something new. Eventually he brought a generator so we had electricity when we needed it. More people came and made little houses. There was a little gully, and one guy from Hawaii made a little arch bridge over it. So our little corner in the woods kept growing and growing and growing, and things were quite nice.

The bus in the middle of the picture is the bus we had. Its location next to the building was nice because I could hear the music or the Bible studies even if I was in the bus taking care of a child.

Drawing 3 shows us during the ATF raid and I am looking over at Jamie by the window and wondering how I can get him. Is this how he dies? Is this how he leaves me? He had gone through so much and we had taken care of him for so long. He was eleven years old then, but at the same time he was still a baby. David said that God sometimes gives us examples of what we would be like if we never grew, if we never improved. He said that perhaps God was giving me an example of this in Jamie to let me know how important it is to grow in Christ. It's an obedience. Children as they grow begin to realize that they should be doing things that are correct because they see it benefits them, and it shows love toward the person who is taking care of them. Jamie's condition helped me to take better care of him, but God also wanted me to see that it's important not to be in a religion and be the same person year after year. Never growing up is a sad, sad situation.

This picture shows Daniel, Kimberly, and me behind the bed, and Jamie is over by the window on a couch. Jamie is screaming because glass has fallen on his face. I would lay Jamie on that couch and he would look out the window. There was enough light for him to know that the light was there, and he could hear the birds. I liked to put him next to the window. Sometimes he would laugh and smile. He would turn his eyes, because he realized it was different there in front of the window than on the other side of the room. He couldn't tell us anything except by the way he acted. He used to laugh a lot when he was younger, but as he got older and toward the time close to when he died, I don't remember him laughing for a long time. He was always crying. When he wasn't crying he was laughing, but then the time came when he was just crying and then he'd be quiet at times.

Drawing 4 shows me with Daniel, Kimberly, and Jamie during the ATF raid. Daniel asks, "Why did the bad men come?" When I first heard the shot, Rachel Sylvia, who lived in the room next door with her mother, brother and sister, ran out of the room. I didn't know what that noise was. I just thought, "I better put them down." We thought that someone had come to talk to David, that's all. We had no idea that all these men were going to be jumping out with guns. This picture shows us together after I pulled Jamie from the couch.

Drawing 5 shows Jaydean Wendell shot dead in her bunk-bed. Her children are on the floor outside the room in the hallway being protected by another woman. These little children were outside lying on the floor while their mother was inside dead. The little brother, the youngest, was five months old and nursing. It was just very sad. I didn't see Jaydean after she was shot. I didn't want to see anyone who was dead.

Drawing 6 shows Daniel and Kimberly sitting in Wayne's office asking, "Where is Daddy?" Wayne's computer and his file cabinet are there. He always had a file cabinet. The picture says that he died on April 19th and he left behind his wife and three children. The picture also reports Wayne's words when he made the 9-1-1 call on February 28 saying that there are women and children here. He's asking them to call off the raid. There are women and children in danger.

Drawing 7 depicts Wayne with little Wayne, Anita, Sheila, Lisa, and Jamie. I put Jamie on Wayne's lap because he sat on his dad's lap. I just wanted to show a picture of them together.

Drawing 8 shows David with the children and it reads, "He loved them all." I wrote all the names of the children who died, seventeen of them, whether they were children that he adopted and treated like his own, or his own children. I wanted people to see that David loved all the children. They didn't have to be his biological children. He loved them and he always encouraged the adults to treat all the children the same way. The little black girl is Melissa Morrison.[89] The dark haired children are the children of Julliette Martinez. Cyrus has the long blonde hair. His sister, Star, has red hair. She's in front of Cyrus. The little one next to Star, in front of David, is Chanel.[90] I put a doll there to show that these were normal children.

I remember watching TV in the Salvation Army halfway house and the reporters asked people: "What do you think about the children?" One guy said, "Oh, if they have to die, let the children die, too." It was so sad. The public didn't see these children. They never touched them. They never talked to them. They were never in their presence.

Drawing 9 shows David laying on the floor in the hallway surrounded by the children and their mothers. The picture says, "March 2nd in hallway." March 2nd was the day when we were going to leave Mount Carmel. David was going to have his tape played over the airwaves and when it was finished we were to go out. From the time he was shot David laid in that hallway on the second floor leading into the east tower. They felt that was the safest place. The red on his side and his wrist are the two places I saw wounds. The women took care of him.

I remember getting our things together in suitcases, and then I waited and waited. All of a sudden I thought, "I need to find out where they went." I went upstairs and David was praying. Everyone was praying so I sat down and we continued to wait. We sat there and listened to a prayer and a Bible study. After it got dark, we started hearing this rumbling and David said those are tanks. He said it would have been better if they had killed us on the first day. Now we are going to be blown to pieces and we will be lying there looking at our body parts. The tanks came onto the property after the FBI agents were told that God had told David to wait and we were not coming out at that time.

In drawing 10 the children are together looking at a newspaper and they ask the oldest child, "Does it say we all died?" The children were always together. They were a family. The child who can read is Cyrus, the little boy with the long blonde hair. He is kind of the tallest and it looks like he's reading. The others are so young they can't read for themselves. They just want to know what happened. In the background is the concrete vault where they died.

I feel such pain for every child who died. Other things happen to people, and because of the tragedy in 1993 I feel the pain of everyone else. The pain is so strong in me that I know that other people feel that horrible emptiness, also. I feel badly when I hear about a little child who has died tragically. I want to love people more, love children more, and to be more compassionate for people.

Drawing 11 says at the bottom, "This was our home!" It shows the building, how it looked before the fire with the water tower, the sand box, the shed, the cafeteria, part of the pool, just to show it was a house. As with other people, David was always trying to fix it up. The seventeen little children who died in the fire are there. At the top of the picture I thought I would show how it looked inside the chapel with the TV, the drums, and David's chair.

Drawing 12 shows the faces of the children who died in the fire and it says, "We didn't want to die." In the left corner of the picture the building at Mount Carmel is on fire. This is my way of saying that all of these little children, all of these faces, why would they want to die? Why would someone want to kill them? I try to remember each one. There were teenagers, too, who died, but at that specific time I decided to show only the faces of the younger ones who died. They didn't want to die.

Drawing 13 depicts toys in a playground with the burning building in the background and a tank in the foreground, and it asks, "Where have all the children gone?" We would look out of the building and see the children playing. There was a tree and toys there. I remember coming out and watching the children day after day. David had bought slides and swings, but we didn't get to put them up. Instead of having a nice playground, the place is on fire and the tank has gone there to destroy the rest. They got rid of the children. They're burning up, so they're saying why should the children have a playground; there are no kids left, so destroy that, too.

Drawing 14 depicts children and their mothers at the pond at Mount Carmel and it reads, "Before 'They' Came." It was a very simple life. The children were happy. They played, had a little pond, fed the geese. It was a very pretty view. Every spring we had beautiful wildflowers. I put flowers in the drawing to show that we had a lot of pretty things to look forward to every spring and summer.

Drawing 15 shows the children playing in the pool and it reads, "Some Times We Remember." That pool was very important to the children. They learned to swim in it. Daniel learned to swim there. When he was just three or four years old he could go under the water.

Drawing 16 is a picture of the children and they're playing and the caption is "We just wanted to play, but. . . ." It shows a tank coming behind them and the building is burning. In this picture I am asking why couldn't they just play? Why did they have to have such short lives? Why did it have to be that way? These children didn't know anything about the FBI and all the things that went on. They should have had a chance. They should have been able to grow up and learn all the things they were supposed to learn.

Drawing 17 shows the children looking at the crape myrtle trees that were planted in memory of each person who died at Mount Carmel in 1993. They see their names on the individual memorial stones underneath the trees. It's like people finding something. One child says, "I think this one is mine." But at the same time these children are not alive; these are signs of death. The trees represent each one who died. It's more than one child. It's two, three, four, five children in one family and four in another. It's just a lot. I feel badly about the fact that those children's names had to be there at all.

Drawing 18 shows the children looking at the large memorial stone at Mount Carmel. One is saying, "Where's your name?" Another child is saying, "Here's mine," another one is saying, "What are all these trees?" and another one is asking, "Where's my toys?" The children are trying to understand what happened. I just wanted to show that this was a sad thing for children to have their names on a stone like that. Their names should be on report cards, birthday cards, things that show they're growing and they're appreciated, not on a stone of death. The trees represent the children and the others who died.

Drawing 19 depicts the faces of the small children with their mothers who died in the vault. The concrete vault surrounded by flames is at the bottom of the picture and it reads, "This is where we all died, April 19th." This is my way of putting a face to the children and their mothers who died. The mothers loved their children. I drew the mothers and their children close to each other, because that's the way it was. The parents all held their children and kept them close during the meetings and eating. We were supposed to take care of our children.

Rachel Howell Koresh (24) is in the right bottom corner of the picture with her three children, Cyrus (8) with the long blonde hair, Star (6) with the reddish hair, and the baby, Bobbie Lane (2). I remember Bobbie as having darker hair. She used to call Lisa's name because Lisa took care of her. Rachel's sister, Michele Jones (18), is in the left bottom corner with Serenity Sea (4) and the twins, Chica and Little One (2). Julliette Martinez (30) is in the center with her five children, Audrey (13), Abigail (11), Joseph (8), Isaiah (8), and Crystal (3). The woman to the left of Julliette Martinez is Judy Schneider (41) with her daughter Mayanah (2). To the right of the Martinez family is Aisha Gyarfas (17) and her daughter Startle (1). To the right of Aisha Gyarfas are Rosemary Morrison (29) and Melissa Morrison (6) from England. Lorraine Sylvia (40) is the woman with the headband in the top left corner of the picture. She always wore her hair like that. Her two daughters Rachel (12) and Hollywood (1) are with her. I knew the Sylvias from Boston so I was extra close to them. Nicole Gent (24) from Australia is in top center of the picture with her two children, Dayland (3) and Paige (1). The redhead in the top right corner of the picture is Kathy Andrade (24) and Chanel (1). Aisha Gyarfas and Nicole Gent were pregnant when they died in the fire.

Drawing 20 is of the people from England who died and it says, "America did this!" Many of them were of Jamaican descent. I don't think they should have had to die. They had a hope of coming over here and learning from the Bible. I wish the people in England had been so angry that they would have demanded an inquiry, but they had the same idea as many Americans, that these were people we didn't need.

Drawing 21 is labeled, "You burn it! We build it!" I drew this after the new chapel was completed at Mount Carmel. Volunteers started building it in September of 1999 and it was dedicated on April 19, 2000. The picture shows the things that were left after the building burned down: the water tower and the concrete vault. Everything else was burned away. The FBI then bulldozed the vault, and the water tower was pulled over.

Drawing 22 entitled "Children Who Lost Parents, April 19th" is a compilation of all the children who survived. This particular drawing came about as I finished other pictures concerning the siege and what happened afterwards and was remembering some of the things that we went through. I started thinking about how many of the surviving children are now in different states and countries. Their parents are not with them because they died. The surviving children have gone to live with other relatives. You know, during the time of the siege, all that was shown in the media was a building and people talking abut the people inside. This way they get to see the children of the parents who died.

Drawing 23 is a composite of three portraits of David Koresh and a unicorn. The unicorn is mentioned in the Bible as having one horn, which symbolizes the male body part. The unicorn represents David because God had anointed him to be the only male who had the right at that time to have children.

Number 24 is a pencil drawing of David with his guitar.

———

When I look at the pictures that I've drawn, especially the one showing my children going out the door and I'm looking at their backs, my first reaction is to think of the hopelessness of their not being around. But the next part of me says that the hope I have is in the Bible where it says we are not to grieve as others do, and that we will see our families again. And then I start to wonder when that will be. When God changes things, am I going to be ready? What is my standing with God? Has the fact of their deaths and the things that have happened helped draw me closer to God? Have I learned something from this experience about how I should treat people?

We were learning obedience the whole time we were with David, for instance, how to listen. We have two ears and one mouth. David was trying to help us to see that we should listen more and speak less.

In all that we went through, the main thing was that we believed in God and kept our faith in him. I am devastated when I see their faces, when remember them, when I think of how they were my babies. I remember the joy and excitement of being pregnant.

I think that speaking to people and making the drawings have helped me relate to this situation and be able to deal with it. One time a person told me that perhaps I should look at the autopsy photographs to help me think of them as really gone. But that was horrible. Who wants to see what happened as a result of these men's minds and actions? It's bad enough to know they are gone, but to have to remember seeing them in such a horribly deformed way. . . . It's enough I know that there were things said in 1993, such as when they told me they'd found pieces of scalp belonging to a certain minority. I didn't know if it was my child or someone else's. I just felt horrible that was all that was left. When I drew the pictures, I remembered the soft skin and the pleasant faces. The happy look on their faces is more important to try to remember than to imagine them burned up.

After a while I was so overwhelmed with so many people that I decided it would be enough to draw only their faces, for example in drawing 25, labeled "Our 23 Children, 1–18 yrs." The children say, "We're gone . . . but not for long." When they come back, they won't look the way we knew them. They will have faces put on them by God, but the Bible says we'll know them.

I'm so very thankful that God gave me wisdom to understand and has guided my hands. I couldn't have done it on my own strength. I feel the Holy Spirit was there to strengthen me and help me do it.

I hope that God sees I've been able to become a better person during these years after the fire. One day it will be all over. These events will just be something I will look back on as part of our lives here on Earth. What happened to us is very small compared to what God is about to do. The comfort I have is in the resurrection—people all over the world coming up and going to heaven. I want to have the experience of seeing all the prophets come together. Scripture says that in the last days we're going to see twenty thousand chariots (Psalm 68:17) waiting to see the last things on Earth, and they're going to come down. I'm looking forward to that. I just hope I'll be someone they will want to have in their home up in heaven. They're coming to live on this Earth, too, so hopefully it will just be an exciting thing. I'm just sorry so much death and bloodshed and horror have to occur on this Earth before something so beautiful happens.

NOTES

1. These papers were published in *New Religious Movements and Religious Liberty in America*, edited by Derek H. Davis and Barry Hankins (Waco, Tex.: Baylor University Press, 2002).

2. Catherine Wessinger, *How the Millennium Comes Violently: From Jonestown to Heaven's Gate* (New York: Seven Bridges Press, 2000). The book's chapters are available on my Web site in pdf format: http://www.loyno.edu/~wessing.

3. They lost the appeal, thus effectively ending the case.

4. The papers by James T. Richardson, Stuart A. Wright, and myself are published in *Waco: Ten Years After, 2003 Fleming Lectures in Religion*, edited by David Tabb Stewart (Georgetown, Tex.: Brown Working Papers in the Arts and Sciences, 2003), available at http://www.southwestern.edu/academic/bwp/pdf/2003bwp-stewart_etal.pdf.

5. On February 28, 1993, four agents of the Bureau of Alcohol, Tobacco, and Firearms (ATF) and five Branch Davidians died as a result of the shootout that occurred as the agents attempted to carry out a "dynamic entry" against the Mount Carmel residence, which is located ten miles east of Waco,

Texas. A sixth Branch Davidian, Michael Schroeder, was shot and killed by ATF agents later that day as he attempted to walk back to Mount Carmel. The agents alleged that he opened fire at them. His body was not retrieved for several days, and Texas Rangers were not permitted by FBI agents to investigate the site during that time. Mount Carmel was surrounded by agents of the Federal Bureau of Investigation, who brought in tanks and waged psychological warfare as their negotiators and the Branch Davidians attempted to communicate with each other. During the fifty-one-day siege, twenty-one children were sent out (including the three youngest Martin children) and fourteen adults came out (including Sheila Martin). The FBI launched a tank and CS gas assault on April 19, 1993, which culminated in the fire that killed seventy-six Branch Davidians including twenty-three children. Two of these children died in utero when their pregnant mothers expired.

6 The Branch Davidians lived in a camp in some woods near Palestine, Texas, from 1985 until 1988, when they returned to Mount Carmel. They were driven off of the Mount Carmel property by the violence of George Roden, the son of the previous prophet, Lois Roden. George, who wanted to be the next prophet, was jealous of the Branch Davidians' allegiance to Vernon Howell, who changed his name to David Koresh in 1990.

 The surviving Branch Davidians, including Sheila, always use the name David or David Koresh, even when referring to periods before he changed his name.

7 After they returned to Mount Carmel in 1988, at first the Branch Davidians lived in separate houses that were already there. In 1991 they began tearing down the houses and using the materials to build the one large residence that became famous in 1993. By spring 1992 most of the community's members had moved into the large house.

8   The ride of Paul Revere and William Dawes from Boston to Lexington took place on April 18–19, 1775, to warn of the approach of British troops. The commemorative poem, "Paul Revere's Ride," was written by Henry Wadsworth Longfellow in 1860, and begins: "Listen my children and you shall hear; Of the midnight ride of Paul Revere. . . ." From 1897 to 1968 the Boston Marathon was held on April 19, Patriot's Day, unless the nineteenth was a Sunday. Since 1969 Patriot's Day has been celebrated on the third Monday in April, and the Boston Marathon is held on that date. See Boston Athletic Association, http://www.bostonmarathon.org/BostonMarathon/RaceFacts.asp, accessed January 4, 2008.

9   The Davidian Seventh-day Adventists were founded as a Seventh-day Adventist splinter group by Victor Houteff in the 1930s. They published a periodical called *The Shepherd's Rod* and other tracts written by Houteff. The Davidians anticipated the imminent restoration of the Davidic messianic kingdom in Palestine (the Holy Land). In May 1935 Houteff moved his group to land purchased outside Waco, Texas, which he named Mount Carmel. They expected the imminent return of Christ, the gathering of the 144,000 to be included in God's kingdom, and their relocation to Palestine, the place where God's kingdom would be set up. Houteff taught that Mount Carmel was where the Davidians would purify themselves in preparation for their admittance into the Promised Land. During the 1940s the Davidians printed their own literature and mailed out as many as 48,000 tracts every two weeks. In the early 1950s, Houteff sent out thirty field workers to spread the Davidian message to Seventh-day Adventists in the United States, Canada, England, India, the West Indies, and Australia.

   Victor Houteff died in 1955 at age 69. Leadership passed to his wife, Florence Houteff. In 1957 she sold the original Mount Carmel property, now on the man-made Lake Waco, and purchased 941 acres ten miles east of Waco, which they also named Mount Carmel. In 1955 Florence announced on the basis of her interpretation of biblical prophecies (Revelation 13:5; Ezekiel 9) that in forty-two months there would be a violent cleansing of the Seventh-day Adventist Church and that the faithful would be transported by God on April 22, 1959, to Palestine where God's kingdom would be set up. Many Davidians gathered at New Mount Carmel in 1959 waiting for these miraculous events. When Florence Houteff's prediction did not materialize, many Davidians left. Florence sold much of the New Mount Carmel property and departed, leaving seventy-seven acres to be purchased by Ben Roden in 1973.

Upon Florence Houteff's departure, Ben Roden was acknowledged as the next prophet after Victor Houteff by a remnant of believers whom he called Branch Davidians. This property was the Mount Carmel that was the site of the violent events involving David Koresh's Branch Davidians in 1993. Ben's wife, Lois Roden, became the next Branch Davidian prophet after his death in 1978.

A young man named Vernon Howell arrived at Mount Carmel in 1981, and Lois indicated that he would succeed her as prophet. Vernon had a spiritual experience in 1985 while he was in Israel, and upon his return he began to teach that he was the Lamb in the New Testament book of Revelation and the endtime messiah possessing the Christ Spirit. In 1990 he changed his name to David Koresh, identifying himself with Cyrus (in Hebrew, Koresh), the king of the Persians who defeated Babylon and liberated the Jews in 539 B.C.E., who in Isaiah 45:1 is called "messiah" (christ). Thus David Koresh indicated that he was the predicted Davidic messiah.

James D. Tabor and Eugene V. Gallagher, *Why Waco? Cults and the Battle for Religious Freedom in America* (Berkeley: University of California Press, 1995), 35, 37–39; Catherine Wessinger, "Autobiographies of Three Surviving Branch

Davidians: An Initial Report," *Fieldwork in Religion* 1, no. 2 (2005): 165–97.

10   Sheila is beginning to adopt the kosher diet and vegetarianism advocated by Ellen G. White, the founding prophet of the Seventh-day Adventist Church.

11   Small pieces of hot dogs baked in biscuits.

12   A *mezuzah* is a parchment on which is written the shema prayer, which is put in a container and affixed to a doorway to secure God's protection. See Deuteronomy 6:4-9, and 11:13-21.

13   Perry Jones, David Koresh's father-in-law, died of wounds he sustained during the shootout with the ATF agents at Mount Carmel on February 28, 1993. He was unarmed and standing behind David Koresh as he met the agents at the front door. He was sixty-four when he died.

14   The Branch Davidians loyal to Vernon Howell (David Koresh) were driven from Mount Carmel by George Roden, the son of Ben and Lois Roden, in 1985. The Branch Davidians constructed a camp on wooded property they purchased near Palestine, Texas. They remained there, living in tents, school buses, and huts until they returned to take possession of Mount Carmel in 1988. The Martin family joined the group at Palestine in 1985, when they first moved to Texas to be with the Branch Davidians there.

15   Novellette Sinclair Hipsman, a Canadian, was thirty-six when she died in the fire on April 19, 1993.

16   In other words, Sheila should not think the observance of Jewish holidays was preparing him to become a Branch Davidian. Ben Roden had instituted the observance of Jewish feast days.

17   The Jewish Sabbath, Shabbat, begins at sunset on Friday and ends at sunset on Saturday. So Jewish businesses and educational institutions cease work before sunset on Friday so that people can observe the commandment not to work on the Sabbath. Seventh-day Adventists and Branch

Davidians observe Saturday as the Sabbath in accordance with the Bible.

18   Among other accusations, George Roden alleged that Vernon Howell (David Koresh) had raped his mother, Lois Roden.

19   In fall 1983 David Koresh, then Vernon Howell, gave a series of Bible studies at Mount Carmel with the title "The Serpent's Root." The intention was to introduce the Branch Davidians to this young man whom Lois Roden was indicating would be her successor to the position of Branch Davidian prophet. Kenneth G. C. Newport, *The Branch Davidians of Waco: The History and Beliefs of an Apocalyptic Sect* (Oxford: Oxford University Press, 2006), 178–79.

20   Branch Davidians see Halloween as a pagan holiday that comes from the devil.

21   Ellen G. White (1827–1915) was the prophet of the Seventh-day Adventist Church. The Branch Davidians believe that the Spirit of Prophecy passed from Sister White to Victor Houteff, the founder of the Davidians, and then to Ben Roden, the founder of the Branch Davidians, and then to Lois Roden and David Koresh. They also believe that the first prophet in this lineage is William Miller (1782–1849), the preacher whose interpretations of the Bible sparked the Millerite movement out of which the Seventh-day Adventist Church emerged. During the Millerite movement, dates were set for Christ's return in 1843 and 1844—the final date, October 22, 1844, became known as "the Great Disappointment."

22   After visiting the community in April 1985 for Passover, Wayne quit his job later in April 1985, bought a school bus, and drove his family to Palestine, Texas. Once there the family lived in the school bus.

23   Vernon (David) had a rock band, which performed his songs that expressed his theology. He visited the music scene in Los Angeles and recruited some young people there to the Branch Davidians, among them David Thibodeau, who was

the drummer in his band. See David Thibodeau and Leon W. Whiteson, *A Place Called Waco: A Survivor's Story* (New York: Public Affairs, 1999). A tape exists of some of David Koresh's songs entitled *Songs to Grandpa* (Gladewater, Tex.: GMC Records, 1996).

24 For instance, Bonnie Haldeman, Vernon's (David's) mother, continued working at her cleaning business after she moved to the Palestine camp in 1985. See Bonnie Haldeman, *Memories of the Branch Daividians: The Autobiography of David Koresh's Mother*, ed. Catherine Wessinger (Waco: Baylor University Press, 2007).

25 In November 1987 George Roden dug up the casket of Anna Hughes, who had been dead for twenty years and was buried at Mount Carmel. Still jealous of Vernon Howell (David Koresh) he challenged Vernon to see which one of them could raise the dead. Vernon reported this to the local sheriff's department, and was told that they would not get involved unless he provided proof that George had dug up the casket. One night Vernon went with some other men, including Stan Sylvia, Paul Fatta, and David Jones, to Mount Carmel to photograph the casket and its contents. They carried weapons since George usually carryied an Uzi semiautomatic weapon. George found them on the property and a shootout ensued. Vernon and the other men were arrested and charged with attempted murder. The other men were acquitted in a trial in April 1988, while the jury could not reach a decision on Vernon Howell. All went free. For a Branch Davidian account of this episode, see Haldeman, *Memories of the Branch Davidians*, 55–59.

26 Lorraine Sylvia ("Larry") was forty when she died in the fire at Mount Carmel on April 19, 1993, with her daughters, Rachel (12) and Hollywood (1).

27 Bonnie Haldeman is David Koresh's mother. She lived with the Branch Davidians from 1985 (the Palestine years) until 1990 (including the return to Mount Carmel).

28   Paul Fatta bailed himself out of jail. The other men stayed in jail until the trial. Paul Fatta (35 in 1993) was not at Mount Carmel when the shootout with the ATF agents occurred. He was subsequently given a fifteen-year sentence for arms violations. He was released from prison in 2005 after serving thirteen and a half years.

29   George Roden was in jail for threatening the judge in the case concerning the shootout at Mount Carmel. Vernon took this opportunity to take control of Mount Carmel. After his release from jail, George Roden murdered a man and was judged insane and confined to a mental hospital. He died of a heart attack at age sixty in 1998 on the grounds of the Big Spring State Hospital in Texas.

30   Kathy Jones grew up at Mount Carmel, and she was married to David Jones, the son of Perry and Mary Belle Jones.

31   Lorraine Sylvia.

32   Ofelia Santoyo's grandchildren at Mount Carmel were the children of her daughter, Julliette Martinez (30). Julie and her five children—Audrey (13), Abigail (11), Joseph (8), Isaiah (4), Crystal (3)—died in the fire.

33   Based on Ezekiel 38 and Zechariah 14, Vernon had taught that the community would relocate to Israel where they would fight with the Israelis against a United Nations force led by the United States in the final battle of Armageddon in 1995. Based on Psalm 89, Isaiah 53, and Revelation 5, he taught that he would be killed in Armageddon, but that he would be resurrected to lead God's army to defeat evil and execute God's judgment. Apparently the plan to get passports to move to Israel did not work out, because in 1993 there was no sign the community was preparing to relocate to the Holy Land. By 1993, with the investigations by Child Protective Services and the ATF, Mount Carmel was stocked with weapons and provisions for a siege. Tabor and Gallagher, *Why Waco?* 76–77; Haldeman, *Memories of the Branch Davidians,* 73.

34   The single men were required to be celibate. Vernon (David) was taking wives from among the younger women to bear his children who were regarded as being God's children with special roles to play in the Endtime events and in God's kingdom.

35   Clive Doyle escaped the fire at Mount Carmel, and currently lives in Waco.

36   Vernon (David) was teaching that the married men and women should also practice celibacy in preparation to receive a true spouse in the kingdom who was part of their souls. He taught that all the women of the community, including the married women, were his wives, and he had children with some of them.

37   Vernon had married Rachel Jones, daughter of Perry and Mary Belle Jones, in 1984 when Rachel was fourteen. Rachel was pregnant with their first child Cyrus when the young couple visited Israel in January 1985. There, Vernon had a spiritual experience that convinced him that he was a prophet, a messiah identified with the statements about Cyrus, the king of the Persians who defeated Babylon, as a messiah in Isaiah, and with the Lamb described in the New Testament book of Revelation. Vernon returned and began teaching his interpretations of the Bible to the Branch Davidians with new confidence and authority. Rachel was twenty-four when she died in the fire in 1993 with her children Cyrus (8), Star (6), and Bobbie Lane (2).

38   Vernon began to take additional wives, with Rachel's permission, in 1986. Rachel agreed because she had a dream instructing her that God wanted Vernon (David) to take additional wives. Haldeman, *Memories of the Branch Davidians*, 43.

39   When the Branch Davidians first returned to Mount Carmel they lived in separate houses.

40   A 1996 movie directed by Ridley Scott.

41   Branch Davidians do not celebrate Christmas, seeing it as a
      pagan holiday originating from Satan.

42   There never was municipal water available at Mount
      Carmel.

43   Woodrow (Bob) and Janet Kendrick were not inside Mount
      Carmel during the violent events in 1993. They were long-
      time Branch Davidians going back to the days of Ben and
      Lois Roden. On February 28, 1993, the day of the ATF
      raid, Bob Kendrick was with Michael Schroeder and Nor-
      man Allison at a Branch Davidian-operated car repair shop
      several miles down the country road. This repair shop was
      dubbed by the media and authorities the "Mag Bag." The
      Mag Bag was in fact a business the Branch Davidians oper-
      ated that involved the women sewing ammunition vests that
      the men sold at gun shows. The Mag Bag mailing address
      was at the car repair shop, hence the misnomer. After the
      shootout at Mount Carmel with the ATF agents, Bob Kend-
      rick, Michael Schroeder, and Norman Allison tried to walk
      back to Mount Carmel. Michael Schroeder was shot and
      killed by AFT agents. Bob Kendrick and Norman Allison
      escaped unharmed but later turned themselves into authori-
      ties. During the 1994 criminal trial, Bob Kendrick, Norman
      Allison, and Clive Doyle were found innocent of all charges.
      Eight other Branch Davidians were convicted on various
      gun charges and seven were convicted of aiding and abet-
      ting voluntary manslaughter.

44   Jaydean Wendel (34) was a former policewoman and appar-
      ently participated in the shootout with the ATF agents on
      February 28, 1993. She received a shot to the head that
      killed her. Her four children, Juanessa (8), Tamara (5),
      Landon (4), and Patron (5 months), were sent out during
      the siege. Her husband, Mark (40), stayed inside and died in
      the fire on April 19.

45   Mary Belle Jones was the wife of Perry Jones. She was not at
      Mount Carmel in 1993 and she continues to live in Waco.

She is the mother of several children, including three who died in the fire: David Jones, Rachel Jones (David's legal wife), and Michele Jones (one of David's extralegal wives).

46   Dana Okimoto, a Japanese American from Hawaii, became one of the wives of David in 1987 when she was twenty. She had two sons, Sky and Scooter, with him. She decided to leave the community when she was at their house in California in 1993 before the conflict at Mount Carmel occurred. Thibodeau and Whiteson, *A Place Called Waco*, n. 111. "Diana Ishikawa" (pseudonym) interviewed in Kenneth Samples, Erwin de Castro, Richard Abanes, and Robert Lyle, *Prophets of the Apocalypse: David Koresh and Other American Messiahs* (Grand Rapids, Mich.: Baker Books, 1994), 182–89, is obviously Dana Okimoto.

47   The large residence included a chapel, a gym, a kitchen, dining room, and an office for Wayne Martin, as well as bedrooms. Men lived on the first floor. Women with children, including Sheila, lived on the second floor. Single women lived on the third floors of the towers on the east and west ends of the building. There was a central tower that included a room for David, but apparently his room was not always located there. There was an arms room in a part of a concrete room at the base of the tower, which had been a vault in the previous building on that site. The concrete vault had survived a fire in 1983 that had consumed the Adminstration Building. Because of the lack of running water at Mount Carmel, elderly women stayed in a trailer down the road where Edna Doyle and Mary Belle Jones looked after them.

48   David had his own rock band consisting of young Branch Davidians recruited mainly in California. David expressed his theology in the songs that he wrote and performed. The lyrics of a couple of his songs can be found in Haldeman, *Memories of the Branch Davidians*, 111–15.

49   Davy Aguilera was the ATF agent who conducted much of
        the investigation into whether or not David Koresh had
        illegal weapons. The investigation began in May 1992. On
        July 23, 1992, Aguilera sent a report to ATF headquarters,
        and the headquarters response was that he had not provided
        enough evidence to justify a search warrant. At that point,
        Aguilera wrote up an affidavit for a warrant alleging that
        the Branch Davidians were a cult that abused children and
        young girls (David was making underage girls his wives), alle-
        gations that did not come under ATF or federal jurisdiction.
        The search warrant for Mount Carmel and the arrest war-
        rant for David Koresh were then authorized by the judge.

        David Koresh and Paul Fatta were engaged in arms trade
        at gun shows to make money to support the approximately
        130 people at Mount Carmel. The allegation was that the
        Branch Davidians were converting semiautomatic weapons
        into automatic weapons without paying the required fees
        for permits to do so. During the investigation, on July 30,
        1992, Aguilera was at the gun shop of Henry McMahon
        interviewing him about his business relationship with
        David Koresh. McMahon got Koresh on the telephone, and
        Koresh, through McMahon, invited the ATF agents to come
        to Mount Carmel openly and inspect his weapons.

        The Branch Davidians were aware that the men who
        moved into one of the houses across the Double E Ranch
        Road from Mount Carmel on January 11, 1993, were federal
        agents of some sort and not the Baylor University students
        they claimed to be. Wessinger, *How the Millennium Comes
        Violently*, 60, 97–98.

50   The reporter with the *Waco Tribune-Herald* would have been
        Mark England. England and Darlene McCormick began
        research in 1992 on stories that became known as the "Sin-
        ful Messiah" series when they appeared in 1993. The series
        was ready for publication in February 1993, but the ATF
        agents asked the *Waco Tribune-Herald* to hold off publishing

it until after they had carried out the "dynamic entry" that they planned to launch against Mount Carmel to deliver warrants. The ATF agents and the *Waco Tribune-Herald* editors then began jockeying to see which side could carry out their respective operations—publishing the articles or launching the raid—first. The first installment of the "Sinful Messiah" series was published on Saturday, February 27, because the editors had concluded that the ATF would conduct the raid on March 1. After the article appeared, the ATF commanders decided to launch their raid the next day, on the morning of February 28.

The first *Waco Tribune-Herald* story by England and McCormick alleged that Koresh had sex with underage girls (true), administered several spankings to babies and little children (this remains disputed and seems to be contradicted by the fond memories that many young people have of their childhood days at Mount Carmel), and that Koresh was accumulating weapons (true). The article painted David Koresh as a "cult leader" and the Branch Davidians, therefore, as "brainwashed cultists."

The presence of *Waco Tribune-Herald* reporters and photographers and cameramen for KWTX-TV in vehicles on the roads just outside Mount Carmel on the morning of February 28 tipped off the Branch Davidians about the impending raid. They were prepared to fight back by the time the ATF agents arrived.

See Catherine Wessinger, "The Branch Davidians and Religion Reporting: A Ten-Year Retrospective," in *Expecting the End: Millennialism in Social and Historical Context*, ed. Kenneth G. C. Newport and Crawford Gribben (Waco, Tex.: Baylor University Press, 2006), 147–72, 270–74.

51 Robert Rodriguez, calling himself Robert Gonzalez, was an undercover agent for the ATF. David Koresh was aware that Rodriguez was an undercover agent of some sort, but he had welcomed him into Mount Carmel, given him Bible stud-

ies, invited him to move in, and shot some of his weapons with him out behind the house. Rodriguez came over early on the morning of February 28 with a copy of that day's *Waco Tribune-Herald* to see if the "Sinful Messiah" series had motivated the Branch Davidians to assume an armed defensive posture at Mount Carmel. While he was with Rodriguez, David Koresh was called out of the room and told that David Jones had learned that a raid was imminent from a cameraman he had encountered on a nearby road.

David Jones was thirty-eight when he died in the fire. His children, Mark (12), Kevin (11), and Heather (9), were sent out during the siege. His estranged wife, Kathy Jones, had already left Mount Carmel.

52   Randy and Vicki Weaver lived with their children in a cabin at Ruby Ridge, Idaho, when Randy, his friend Kevin Harris, and his son Sammy (14) got into a gun fight with federal marshals who had them under surveillance. After the marshals shot his dog, Sammy pointed his rifle at them. The marshals opened fire and killed Sammy. Randy Weaver and Kevin Harris retreated to the cabin. The cabin was subsequently surrounded by FBI agents who did not announce their presence and did not warn them that they had been given "rules of engagement" to shoot any armed male adult they saw. FBI agents opened fire when Randy Weaver and Kevin Harris came out of the cabin, striking and killing Vicki Weaver while holding her baby as she held the door open for the men. "Ruby Ridge" became a synonym for heavy-handed and unjust tactics carried out by federal agents against American citizens.

53   Catherine Matteson was seventy-seven in 1993. She was a long-time Branch Davidian who had joined during the days of Ben and Lois Roden. She was Lois Roden's right-hand woman in managing the business of the community. She along with other key Branch Davidians had shifted their allegiance to Vernon Howell in 1984–1985, believing that

Lois had lost the "Spirit of Prophecy," and that Vernon was the next Branch Davidian prophet. On Lois Roden losing the Spirit of Prophecy, see Matteson Tape #2, recorded in Catherine Matteson's home in Waco on October 11, 2004.

Catherine Matteson was sent out of Mount Carmel by David Koresh on March 2 along with Margaret Lawson (75), and Daniel (6) and Kimberly (4) Martin. Catherine carried out an audiotape made by the wounded David Koresh in which he explained his theology. He had made a deal with federal agents that if the tape was played on network television they would come out. The Branch Davidians prepared to exit Mount Carmel after the tape was played on KRLD radio and the Christian Broadcasting Network, but at 4:00 p.m. Koresh announced that he was instructed by God to wait. From that point on, most of the Branch Davidians remained inside waiting to see what God's will for them would be.

Jamie Martin (11) and Joshua Sylvia (7) were sent out earlier on March 2, becoming the first children to be sent out of Mount Carmel.

54 Sheila's room, which she shared with Jamie, Daniel, and Kimberly, was on the front east corner on the second floor above the front doors of the residence. Wayne Martin's office was on the first floor just below Sheila's room.

55 Robert Rodriguez drove across the street to the undercover house and called his commanders and begged them to call off the raid because the "element of surprise" had been lost. Instead the commanders told the seventy-six armed agents to hurry up and carry out the raid. The search warrant did not authorize a "no-knock" raid, but they had received training by Special Forces at Fort Hood to carry out such a raid on Mount Carmel.

56 The ATF agents were driven up to the front door in cattle trailers.

57   ATF agents Todd McKeehan (28), Conway Lebleu (36), Robert Williams (27), and Steve Willis (32) were killed during the shootout.

58   Michele Jones was Rachel Jones' younger sister. She had become one of David Koresh's wives in 1987 when she was twelve. Michele was eighteen in 1993. She had three children by David: Serenity Sea (4 in 1993), and twins, Chica and Little One (age 2 in 1993). They all died in the fire on April 19.

59   Sheila explained that this referred to the people of Israel who were led out of Egypt by Moses, but who were led into Canaan by Joshua and Caleb. All the adults who had left Egypt with Moses had died by the time the Israelites entered the promised land. Joshua and Caleb were the only Israelites over age twenty who entered into Canaan after the exodus from Egypt and the forty years of wandering.

       Sheila said that Perry Jones and Clive Doyle and other adults who were parents and grandparents used to remark that the Branch Davidian children would not have to go through the rebellious teenage years as did other children, because the Branch Davidian children would be in the kingdom—which would be an earthly kingdom—by the time they were teenagers. The Branch Davidian children would not "leave the message" or "backslide." God would use the young people to "hold up the truth" (telephone conversation with Sheila Martin on June 5, 2008).

60   When the shooting started, Wayne Martin dialed 9-1-1 and got the sheriff's office. He shouted into his speakerphone asking that the shooting stop:

            MARTIN: Yeah, there are seventy-five men around our building and they're shooting at us in Mt. Carmel!
            LYNCH: Mt. Carmel?
            MARTIN: Yeah. Tell them there are children and women in here and to call it off!

Wayne also did a lot of shouting to communicate with the Branch Davidian men and with the sheriff's office on his speakerphone, as he negotiated a ceasefire between the Branch Davidians and the ATF agents. This portion of the 9-1-1 call is quoted in Wessinger, *How the Millennium Comes Violently*, 68; David Hardy discusses Wayne's role in arranging the ceasefire in David T. Hardy with Rex Kimball, *This Is Not an Assault: Penetrating the Web of Official Lies Regarding the Waco Incident* (n.p.: Xlibris Corporation, 2001), 228–36.

61   The Branch Davidians believed that these events may have meant that they were in the Fifth Seal of the book of Revelation, which they believed predicted the Endtime events. Koresh stated in his message broadcast on KRLD radio on February 28: "We are now in the Fifth Seal." The book of Revelation speaks of a scroll or a book sealed with Seven Seals. Only the Lamb, whom the Branch Davidians believed was David Koresh, could open or interpret the Seven Seals and bring about their events. The events predicted in each of the Seven Seals related to the catastrophic occurrences of the Endtime leading to God's judgment and the creation of his kingdom for the faithful. The Fifth Seal in Revelation 6:9-11 in the King James Version of the Bible reads:

> And when he had opened the fifth seal, I saw under the altar the souls of them that were slain for the word of God, and for the testimony which they held; and they cried out with a loud voice, saying, How long, O Lord, holy and true, dost thou not judge and avenge our blood on them that dwell on the earth? And white robes were given unto every one of them; and it was said unto them, that they should rest yet for a little season, until their fellow-servants also and their brethren, that should be killed as they were, should be fulfilled.

Five Branch Davidians died as a result of the shootout with the ATF: Perry Jones (64), Peter Hipsman (28), Winston Blake (28), Peter Gent (24), and Jaydean Wendel (34).

Michael Schroeder (29) was shot and killed by ATF agents later in the day as he attempted to walk back to Mount Carmel. The ATF agents alleged that he had fired upon him, but federal agents' lack of care to preserve the evidence relating to his death raises many questions.

The Branch Davidians believed that they might be in the Fifth Seal, in which some of the faithful are killed by agents of the Satan-dominated system that the book of Revelation calls "Babylon," and that after a waiting period, the rest of the faithful community would be killed by Babylon, after which they would be resurrected and fight in the Lamb's army to destroy evil, bring God's judgment, and then become honored members of God's kingdom.

David Koresh was interpreting the events at Mount Carmel in light of his interpretations of the biblical prophecies. His interpretations were not set in stone. They responded to events and actions of the federal agents. Beginning on March 2 when Koresh received God's order to "wait," the Branch Davidians were waiting to see whether or not they really were in the Fifth Seal. Negotiation transcripts reveal that they did not want to die at that time, and they attempted to negotiate with the FBI agents who took charge of the fifty-one-day siege. But most of the Branch Davidians would not come out unless they thought that it would conform to God's will as revealed in the Bible. They were open to receiving input from Bible scholars about alternative interpretations, but they were adamant that their actions should be in accordance with the biblical prophecies. Tabor and Gallagher, *Why Waco?*; Jayne Seminare Docherty, *Learning Lessons from Waco: When the Parties Bring Their Gods to the Negotiation Table* (Syracuse: Syracuse University Press, 2001); Eugene V. Gallagher, "'Theology Is Life and Death': David Koresh on Violence, Persecution, and the Millennium," in *Millennialism, Persecution, and Violence: Historical Cases*, ed.

Catherine Wessinger (Syracuse: Syracuse University Press, 2000), 82–100; Wessinger, *How the Millennium Comes Violently*, 56–119.

62 This is the audiotape that David sent out with Catherine Matteson to be played on television, and which was played on KRLD radio and the Christian Broadcasting Network on March 2, Tuesday. David had agreed that they would come out after his audiotaped sermon was played in the media.

63 Some Branch Davidians alleged that ATF agents in the three National Guard helicopters that circled over the residence shot down at them. The ATF agents denied this.

64 Catherine Matteson, whose room was on the back of the building, said that she saw agents shooting from helicopters. Catherine Matteson's unpublished memoirs recorded in 1994 and transcribed by Mark Swett reports her account of the February 28 raid, that she saw shots being fired from the helicopters:

> As I crossed the floor, I noticed as I looked out the two windows two cattle car-trailers coming down the road toward the house. My thoughts were, what were the men going to do with these large trailers? I left the foyer, ran down the hall to the back stairs, ran up stairs thinking it will be nice to lie down and read what was printed in the [news]paper. All the while [I was] wondering what could be said in seven articles that would be of interest to the readers. In my room I threw the paper on my bed and started to lay down when the loud sound of helicopters roared in my ears. They sounded as if they were in the room with me. My room was at the back of the building on the second floor. As I went to the window to my amazement there were three helicopters in formation facing David's room and firing as they came. As the helicopters came near the building they were between the second and third floor level. They were coming between the water tower and the

north corner of the building. I felt as if I could touch them. As the helicopters came near the building they were between the second and third floor level. There were no other shots being fired before or during this happening. David's room projected out from the other side of the building. There were no other rooms in that area. The shots from the helicopters could be clearly heard and seen. This was the closest a plane or flying helicopter had ever come near me. It was like looking at a movie only it was real. As they made a turn toward the front of the building I realized there existed a great possibility of my getting shot so I hit the floor. When they reached the front of the building all hell broke loose and everyone at the front of the building started shooting. What I saw was verified by Margie [Margorie Thomas] when she was interviewed by the government. She was the one who had 80 degree burns. She went back to England.

Margie lived on the third floor in the short tower on [the] north side. The helicopters were closer to her room because I lived three rooms down from the north corner. When she heard the noise it was as if they were in her room also. As she looked out she saw legs hanging out of the helicopters. She saw them shooting and heard the rapid fire of the shots. Margie had 80 percent of her body burned. She did go back to England. At the grand jury they asked me if I had seen anyone in the helicopters but I had not. When I saw the helicopters I was looking at the front of them. When Margie saw the helicopters they had already turned toward the front of the building and she saw the side with the door open and the men sitting in the open doorway. They were going along the north side of our building to the front. Colonel Jack Zimmerman [one of the Branch Davidians' defense attorneys in the 1994 criminal trial] was able to see the damage they did to David's room. There were bullet holes everywhere. It looked like Swiss cheese. He told them that in court.

65   The FBI negotiators sent in a videotape of the children who were sent out of Mount Carmel and who had been taken to the Methodist Children's Home. Their intention was to demonstrate to the Branch Davidians that the children were well cared for. The videotape had the opposite effect, since it showed the children jumping around in an undisciplined manner, and the mothers were concerned that they were being fed junk food containing a lot of sugar.

On March 8, the Branch Davidians sent to the negotiators a videotape of the severely wounded David Koresh introducing the children in his family as well as their mothers. On March 9, the Branch Davidians sent out another videotape in which the adults explained why they were waiting on God. The FBI did not release the Branch Davidians' videotapes to the media as the Branch Davidians wished. The Branch Davidians were erased as individuals in the media to a great extent, because the media focused on depicting David Koresh as a crazy and manipulative "cult leader." The Branch Davidians realized that they were being dehumanized in the media, and on March 9 they hung a sheet out one of the windows on which was written, "God Help Us We Want the Press." Wessinger, *How the Millennium Comes Violently*, 72.

66   Catherine Wessinger obtained her copy through scholars who had obtained the combined Branch Davidian videotapes on one video cassette provided by the Branch Davidians' defense attorneys. This videotape has been circulated with the title "Inside Mount Carmel."

67   News reporters were pushed back to a site three miles from Mount Carmel.

68   Steve Schneider was a former Seventh-day Adventist who had earned a Master's Degree in religious studies from the

University of Hawaii. He was the person who did most of the negotiating with FBI agents during the siege, and he functioned as David's right-hand man. He was also a skilled and enthusiastic teacher of David's doctrines. Steve was 43 when he died in the fire.

69   The FBI agents punished the Branch Davidians every time adults came out. This can be seen clearly in an "interpretive log" compiled by James Tabor. See James Tabor, "The Events at Waco: An Interpretative Log," http://home.maine. rr.com/waco/ww.html, now defunct; the interpretive log is currently located at http://ccat.sas.upenn.edu/gopher/text/ religion/koresh/Koresh%20Log, accessed January 28, 2005.

    Sheila came out on March 21 with the largest group of adults to exit at one time. She came out with Victorine Hollingsworth (58), Anetta Richards (64), Rita Riddle (35), Gladys Ottman (67), James Lawter (70), and Ofelia Santoyo (62). Then the FBI began blasting high decibel sounds at the Branch Davidians. David Koresh and Steve Schneider angrily said that the Branch Davidians who were planning to come out had decided not to. During the following days, the FBI agents blasted sounds of helicopters, dentists' drills, bagpipes, sirens, dying rabbits, Tibetan Buddhist chants, Muslim prayer calls, Christmas carols, songs by Alice Cooper, and Nancy Sinatra singing "These Boots Are Made for Walkin'."

70   Lisa moved up to the third floor in the tower right before the events on February 28, 1993.

71   By that time, Byron Sage was the primary FBI negotiator working with the Branch Davidians.

72   "Cult Children of the Damned," *National Inquirer*, April 20, 1993.

73   CS gas, chlorobenzylidene maloninitrile, was the tear gas being inserted into the building through nozzles on the booms of the tanks and by ferret rounds fired into the building. The tanks also drove into the building and began dismantling it. CS gas belongs to a family of "riot control"

agents that cause "acute irritation to the eyes, mouth, nose, and upper respiratory tract. . . ." It was designed for use outdoors to control people. It was not originally intended for use in enclosed spaces. It irritates the nasal passages, mouth, eyes, respiratory system in general, and even the stomach. It burns the skin. The 1996 congressional report on the events at Mount Carmel concluded: "CS insertion into the enclosed bunker [the concrete room] at a time when women and children were assembled inside that enclosed space could have been a proximate cause of or directly resulted in some or all of the deaths attributed to asphyxiation in the autopsy reports." The methylene chloride that was used with the CS gas as a disbursant has an anaesthetic effect and that chemical "might have impaired the ability of some of the [Branch] Davidians to be able to leave the residence had they otherwise wished to do so." House of Representatives, *Investigation into the Activities of Federal Law Enforcement Agencies toward the Branch Davidians*, Report 104-749 (Washington, D.C.: U.S. Government Printing Office, 1996), 69–75, quotations on 69, 71, 75.

74   A flame appeared in the window of Sheila's room on the front east corner of the building at 12:07 p.m. At 12:08 a fire could be seen in the dining area. At 12:08 another fire could be seen in the gym, where the entering tanks had caused the roof to collapse.

75   This was the contention of the video, *Waco: The Rules of Engagement* produced by Dan Gifford, William Gazecki, and Michael McNulty (Los Angeles: Fifth Estate Productions, 1997).

    The Rules of Engagement depicts Dr. Edward F. Allard, an expert in Forward Looking Infrared (FLIR) technology analyzing FLIR film that was shot from an airplane circling over Mount Carmel at the time of the tank and gas assault and concluding that flashes on the ground represented gunfire being directed toward the residence.

This allegation was contested by the government in the 2000 wrongful death civil trial. A "reenactment" of the conditions of the assault were conducted at Fort Hood as part of the trial proceedings, and the government's experts concluded that the flashes were too short to be gunfire, but they were instead light reflecting off of objects on the ground. Also, the government argued that if there were shooters, they would have shown up on the FLIR tapes. The plaintiffs' FLIR experts contended that the flashes were indeed gunfire and that two men could be faintly seen on the FLIR tapes moving about firing weapons.

Michael McNulty, one of the producers of *Waco: The Rules of Engagement*, carried out his own FLIR experiment and concluded that gun flashes caught by FLIR tape were indeed the length of the flashes seen on the April 19 FLIR tape recorded above Mount Carmel. McNulty's third video on the Branch Davidian case, *The F.L.I.R. Project*, producer Michael McNulty (Fort Collins, Colo.: COPS Productions, n.d.), presents the results of his FLIR experiment.

In November 2000, former United States Senator John Danforth, who had been designated special counsel by Attorney General Janet Reno to investigate whether federal agents had engaged in wrongdoing at Mount Carmel, published his report concluding that federal agents did not fire at the Branch Davidians on April 19, 1993.

Hardy, *This Is Not an Assault*, 148–52; "Declaration of Edward F. Allard, Ph.D.," *Deborah Brown, et al. v. United States of America, et al.*, United States District Court, Southern District of Texas, Houston Division, Civil Action No. H95-587, at http://news.findlaw.com/hdocs/docs/waco/allard_affidavit.html, accessed October 24, 2005; John C. Danforth, Special Counsel, "Final Report to the Deputy Attorney General concerning the 1993 Confrontation at the Mt. Carmel Complex, Waco, Texas," November 8, 2000, at http://www.apologeticsindex.org/pdf/finalreport.pdf, accessed October 24, 2005; Jean E. Rosenfeld, "The Use of the Military at Waco: The Danforth Report in Context," *Nova Religio: The Journal of Alternative and Emergent Religions* 5, no. 1 (2001): 171–85.

76 Shari Doyle was eighteen when she died in the fire.

77 Misty Ferguson (17) suffered severe burns on her hands, and her fingers had to be amputated. Marjorie Thomas (30) suffered severe burns over half of her body. Ruth Riddle (29) suffered a broken ankle and burns. FBI agents pulled Ruth away from the fire after she jumped from the second floor.

78 Derek Lovelock (37), Jaime Castillo (24), David Thibodeau (24), and Clive Doyle (52) escaped through a hole that a tank had punched into the wall of the chapel. Renos Avraam (29) jumped from the second floor. Graeme Craddock (31) survived by hiding in a cinder block structure next to the water tower.

79 Bonnie Haldeman also reports that David taught the parents never to spank the children out of anger but only in order to discipline them. See Haldeman, *Memories of the Branch Davidians*, 21.

80 Janet McBean was out in California during the violent events at Mount Carmel. Her brother, John-Mark McBean (27), died in the fire.

81 David Thibodeau also reported his impressions of the Maury Povich show in Thibodeau and Whiteson, *A Place Called Waco*, 303–7.

82 Eleven Branch Davidians were tried in the criminal trial in 1994 in San Antonio. Clive Doyle was acquitted of charges of conspiracy to murder federal agents, aiding and abetting the murder of federal agents, and carrying a weapon during the commission of a violent crime. Norman Allison and Woodrow Kendrick were also acquitted of all charges.

Seven Branch Davidians were convicted of aiding and abetting voluntary manslaughter; five Branch Davidians were found guilty of carrying a firearm during the commission of a violent crime; and two Branch Davidians were found guilty of other arms violations. The jury forewoman later said that the jury's intent with their verdicts was to indicate that they found fault on both sides of the conflict. United States District Judge Walter Smith Jr. imposed excessively lengthy sentences on the convicted Branch Davidians that were later overturned by the Supreme Court, which directed Judge Smith to impose standard sentences. Renos Avraam, Kevin Whitecliff, Brad Branch, Jaime Castillo, Paul Fatta, and Graeme Craddock were released in 2006. Livingstone Fagan was released in 2007. Craddock was deported to Australia, and Avraam and Fagan were deported to Britain. Ruth Riddle was sentenced to five years for possessing a firearm during the shootout. Kathy Schroeder, a witness for the prosecution, was separately sentenced to three years in prison.

Edna Doyle, Clive Doyle's mother, passed away in 2001.

83   The freezer at the Tarrant County medical examiner's office mysteriously malfunctioned and permitted the bodies to decompose. The exact circumstances of this event have not been adequately investigated. The medical examiner's office said that the cooler kept the bodies in temperatures in the low 40s instead of the mid-thirties (Fahrenheit), thus they turned into "soup." The cooler contained at least one body, that of Perry Jones, for which the autopsy results were in dispute. The Branch Davidians reported that Perry Jones was mortally wounded by the gunfire as he stood at the front door right behind David Koresh, as Koresh attempted to speak to the armed ATF agents rushing up to the residence. Branch Davidian Kathy Schroeder testified that after he was shot in the abdomen Perry begged to be put out of his misery and that Neil Vaega (who died in the fire on April 19) delivered the gunshot that killed him. The coroner reported

finding only a single bullet wound in Perry's body, fired at pointblank range, into the roof of his mouth. With all the bodies in the cooler turned into soup, it was impossible to reexamine Perry Jones' body to settle the dispute. See Dick J. Reavis, *Ashes of Waco: An Investigation* (New York: Simon & Schuster, 1995), 146–49.

84   The Branch Davidian children (15 and younger) who died on April 19, 1993, buried at the paupers' field, are Cyrus Howell Koresh (8); Star Howell Koresh (6); Bobbie Lane Koresh (2); Serenity Sea Jones (4); Chica and Little One Jones (2); Lisa Marie Martin (13); Sheila Renee Martin (15); Melissa Morrison (6); and the children of Julliette Martinez: Audrey Martinez (13); Abigail Martinez (11); Joseph Martinez (8); Isaiah Barrios (4); and Crystal Barrios (3).

85   The surviving family members were not consulted about the names of their loved ones buried in the paupers' cemetery when the small marble markers were made. Many of the names are listed as "Unknown."

86   The small children and their mothers took refuge in a concrete vault at the base of the central tower when the tank and CS gas assault began. Of the twenty-three children aged fifteen and under who died on April 19, 1993, eighteen were eight years old or under, including two infants who died in utero.

87   Ron Howard directed the 1991 movie *Backdraft*.

88   The flames appeared in the window of Sheila's room on the second floor of the east corner at 12:07 p.m. By 12:08 a fire was seen in the dining room. Also at 12:08 another fire was seen in the gym where tanks had collapsed the roof. At 12:13 FBI agents called the fire department. Fire trucks arrived at 12:34, but Jeffrey Jamar, the FBI Special Agent in Charge, held the fire trucks back, later saying it was to prevent the firefighters from being shot by the Branch Davidians. At 12:41, with the residence completely burned down, the firefighters were permitted to spray water on the hot ashes. See

photographs in this volume taken from the government's exhibits in the 2000 wrongful death civil lawsuit.

89   Melissa Morrison was six and her mother, Rosemary Morrison, was twenty-nine when they died in the fire. They were from Britain.

90   Chanel Andrade was one, and her mother, Kathy Andrade, was twenty-four, when they died in the fire. Kathy's younger sister, Jennifer (20), also died in the fire.

WORKS CITED

Allard, Edward F. [2005.] "Declaration of Edward F. Allard, PhD." *Deborah Brown, et al. v. United States of America, et al.* United States District Court, Southern District of Texas, Houston Division, Civil Action No. H95-587. http://news.findlaw.com/hdocs/docs/waco/allard_affidavit.html. Accessed October 24.

"Cult Children of the Damned." 1993. *National Inquirer,* April 20.

Danforth, John, Special Council. 2000. "Final Report to the Deputy Attorney General Concerning the 1993 Confrontation at the Mt. Carmel Complex, Waco, Texas, November 8, 2000 Pursuant to Order No. 2256-99 of the Attorney General." Available at http://www.apologeticsindex.org/pdf/finalreport.pdf.

Davis, Derek. H., and Barry Hankins, eds. 2002. *New Religious Movements and Religious Liberty in America.* Waco, Tex.: Baylor University Press, 2002.

Docherty, Jayne Seminare. 2001. *Learning the Lessons from Waco: When the Parties Bring Their Gods to the Negotiation Table*. Syracuse: Syracuse University Press.

Gallagher, Eugene V. 2000. "'Theology Is Life and Death': David Koresh on Violence, Persecution, and the Millennium." In *Millennialism, Persecution, and Violence: Historical Cases*, ed. Catherine Wessinger, 82–100. Syracuse: Syracuse University Press.

Gifford, Dan, William Gazecki, and Michael McNulty, producers. 1997. "Waco: The Rules of Engagement." Los Angeles: Fifth Estate Productions.

Haldeman, Bonnie. 2007. *Memories of the Branch Daividians: The Autobiography of David Koresh's Mother*. Edited by Catherine Wessinger. Waco: Baylor University Press.

Hardy, David T., with Rex Kimball. 2001. *This Is Not an Assault: Penetrating the Web of Official Lies Regarding the Waco Incident*. N.p.: Xlibris Corporation.

House of Representatives. 1996. *Investigation into the Activities of Federal Law Enforcement Agencies toward the Branch Davidians: Thirteenth Report by the Committee on Government Reform and Oversight Prepared in Conjunction with the Committee on the Judiciary together with Additional and Dissenting Views*. Report 104-749. Washington, D.C.: U.S. Government Printing Office.

Koresh, David. 1996. *Songs to Grandpa*. Gladewater, Tex.: GMC Records. Audiotape.

Matteson, Catherine. 2004. Tape #2. Interview with Catherine Matteson in Waco, Texas on October 11.

McNulty, Michael, producer. 2001. "The F.L.I.R. Project." Fort Collins, Colo.: COPS Productions.

Newport, Kenneth G. C. 2006. *The Branch Davidians of Waco: The History and Beliefs of an Apocalyptic Sect.* Oxford: Oxford University Press.

Reavis, Dick J. 1995. *The Ashes of Waco: An Investigation.* New York: Simon & Schuster, 1995.

Rosenfeld, Jean E. 2001. "The Use of the Military at Waco: The Danforth Report in Context." *Nova Religio: The Journal of Alternative and Emergent Religions* 5, no. 1: 171–85.

Samples, Kenneth, Erwin de Castro, Richard Abanes, and Robert Lyle. 1994. *Prophets of the Apocalypse: David Koresh and Other American Messiahs.* Grand Rapids, Mich.: Baker Books.

Stewart, David Tabb, ed. 2003. *Waco: Ten Years After, 2003 Fleming Lectures in Religion.* Georgetown, Tex.: Brown Working Papers in the Arts and Sciences. Available at http://www.southwestern.edu/academic/bwp/pdf/2003bwp-stewart_etal.pdf.

Tabor, James D. [2005.] "The Events at Waco: An Interpretative Log." http://ccat.sas.upenn.edu/gopher/text/religion/koresh/Koresh%2Log. Accessed January 28.

Tabor, James D., and Eugene V. Gallagher. 1995. *Why Waco? Cults and the Battle for Religious Freedom in America.* Berkeley: University of California Press.

Thibodeau, David, and Leon W. Whiteson. 1999. *A Place Called Waco: A Survivor's Story.* New York: Public Affairs.

Wessinger, Catherine. 2000. *How the Millennium Comes Violently: From Jonestown to heaven's Gate.* New York: Seven Bridges Press. Available at http://www.loyno.edu/~wessing.

———. 2005. "Autobiographies of Three Surviving Branch Davidians: An Initial Report." *Fieldwork in Religion* 1, no. 2: 165–97.

———. 2006. "The Branch Davidians and Religion Reporting: A Ten-Year Retrospective." In *Expecting the End: Millennialism in Social and Historical Context*, ed. Kenneth G. C. Newport and Crawford Gribben, 147–72, 270–74. Waco, Tex.: Baylor University Press.

INDEX